The Official Gift in Ancient Egypt

The Official Gift in Ancient Egypt

By Edward Bleiberg

University of Oklahoma Press : Norman and London

Library of Congress Cataloging-in-Publication Data

Bleiberg, Edward, 1951–
The official gift in ancient Egypt / by Edward Bleiberg.
p. cm.
Includes bibliographical references and index.
ISBN 0-8061-2871-2 (alk. paper)
1. Egypt—Economic conditions—To 332 B.C. 2. Gifts—Egypt—History. 3. Inw (The Egyptian word). I. Title.
HC33.B57 1996
932′.01—dc20 96–20282
CIP

Text design by Cathy Carney Imboden.

The paper in this book meets the guidelines for permanence and durability of the Committee on Production Guidelines for Book Longevity of the Council on Library Resources, Inc. ♾

1 2 3 4 5 6 7 8 9 10

Contents

Preface	vii
Acknowledgments	xi
List of Abbreviations	xiii
Chapter One. The Setting for Exchanges of *Inw*	3
Chapter Two. The Emergence and Development of *Inw* Exchanges during the Archaic Period and the Old Kingdom	29
Dynasty 1	29
Dynasty 2	35
Dynasty 3	38
The Old Kingdom: Dynasties 5 and 6	42
Conclusions About *Inw* in the First Six Dynasties	51
Chapter Three. *Inw* during the First Intermediate Period and the Middle Kingdom: A Broadening Concept	54
The First Intermediate Period	55
The Early Middle Kingdom	56
Dynasty 12	64
Inw at the Royal Center in Dynasties 12 and 13	74

Excursus on *Inw* as Products in Literature 86
Conclusions about *Inw* in the First Intermediate Period and the Middle Kingdom 87
Chapter Four. *Inw* in the New Kingdom: The View from Monumental Inscriptions 90
Inw as the Royal Privy-Purse 90
The Uses of *Inw* 100
The Administration of *Inw* in the New Kingdom 103
Conclusions about *Inw* in the New Kingdom 114
Chapter Five. Conclusions: Evidence, Bias, Models 115
Appendix. Translations of *Inw* 126
Notes 131
Bibliography 153
Index of Egyptian Sources 165
General Index 167

Preface

This book is both a chronological study and a methodological experiment. First, it is a chronological study of *inw,* an Egyptian designation for one kind of commodity exchange. Its literal meaning, "that which is brought," has been rendered by Egyptologists with numerous words in European languages. Each translation has been an ad hoc response to a specific context where the word has been found. (See the appendix for the variety of translations that have been offered.)

The most basic intention of this study is to discover the unifying concept that motivated the Egyptians to describe with one word what appears to modern scholars as a variety of types of exchanges. Once I began my research, it became clear to me that the difficulty Egyptologists experienced in equating the Egyptian word with one modern economic concept could be located in the basic differences between the Egyptian economy and an industrial economy. This problem thus lends itself well to testing Jac. J. Janssen's application of Karl Polanyi's model of the redistributive economy to ancient Egypt over an extended time period. As we will see, Janssen's understanding of the Egyptian economy as an example of a redistributive economic system can be verified and expanded through explaining the place of *inw*-exchanges within it from the beginnings of Egyptian history until Ramesside times. This work thus begins with an examination of arguments for and against applying the redistributive model to Egypt. It argues in favor of Janssen's view but expands it to include the earlier periods as well as the Ramesside Period. It continues with three studies of *inw* arranged chronologically, each outlining the role of these exchanges during the major periods of Bronze Age Egyptian history. A concluding chapter ties together the history of these exchanges from Archaic through Ramesside times.

The second, somewhat broader problem addressed here is methodological. Tracing one phenomenon through third- and second-millennium B.C. Egyptian history remains difficult, given the uneven preservation of the sources. This problem is basic to writing ancient Egyptian history of any variety—political, literary, social, or economic. It is not always clear whether a unique attestation of a phenomenon could have been typical or whether generalizations can be formulated from the presence or absence of that same phenomenon in a subsequent or previous time period. Generalizing from unique, limited, or absent data also assumes more accurate knowledge than we usually possess. It more often reveals a gap between modern expectations of the next logical step and the real chance that this "logical expectation" would never have occurred to the ancients. Yet most scholars explicitly or implicitly use a model or mental template in weighing the evidence and arranging it into a meaningful whole. This model is often based on contemporary Western society, especially when it considers practical matters, such as the economy. Here an attempt has been made to be very explicit about the nature of the model before using it to arrange the data and fill in the gaps. It also looks to other preindustrial societies to formulate the mental template of likely and unlikely events by using a model borrowed from economic anthropology. It posits the importance of social relations in a redistributive, preindustrial economy. Once the model is formulated in chapter 1, the chronological studies consider the reliability of the model for describing this aspect of the Egyptian economy. The conclusion also considers the successes and failures of this method of writing Egyptian history.

I hope that both the explanation of *inw* as an "official gift" and this example of modeling as a methodological approach will serve as evidence for the validity of this technique for writing the history of ancient Egypt.

Acknowledgments

This book was written over the course of six years, mostly during summer vacations. I owe a debt of gratitude to the National Endowment for the Humanities, which supported this work through a Summer Stipend in 1987 and a Travel to Collections Grant in 1990. I am also grateful to the American Council of Learned Societies, which supported research done during the summer of 1988 through a Grant-in-Aid. Financial support for this work was also derived through a Faculty Research Leave from the University of Memphis in the fall semester of 1992. I am grateful to Richard R. Ranta, the dean of the College of Communication and Fine Arts at the University of Memphis, for his support in obtaining leave time to complete this work. I also thank Carol J. Crown and Robert E. Lewis, previous and current chairs of the Department of Art, for their support.

Thanks is also due for access to archives made possible by Jaromir Málek, Griffith Institute, Oxford; Ingeborg Müller, Staatliche Museen, Berlin; Dorothea Arnold and Marsha Hill, Metropolitan Museum, New York; and Alessandro Roccati, then at the Museo Egizio, Turin.

This work has also benefited over the years from discussions with David Berg, Donald B. Redford, and Donald Spanel. Special thanks to Betsy M. Bryan and Ronald J. Leprohon for careful and enormously helpful readings of the manuscript. I thank all of them for their time and intelligence applied to problems that I have proposed. Naturally, I accept full responsibility for any errors found here.

I also wish to thank Richard Fazzini and James Romano of the Brooklyn Museum and the staff of the Wilbour Library, especially Diane Bergman and Mary Gow, both for making me feel so welcome during the fall of 1992 and for putting at my disposal the resources of the Wilbour Library.

Finally, many thanks to Mrs. Annette Lane, Secretary at the Institute of Egyptian Art and Archaeology, for her aid and skill in word processing the typescript more than once.

Abbreviations

AEL	M. Lichtheim, *Ancient Egyptian Literature,* 3 vols. Berkeley, 1976
AEO	A. Gardiner, *Ancient Egyptian Onomastica,* London, 1947
AoF	*Altorientalishe Forschungen,* Berlin
APAW	Abhandlungen der Preußischen Akademie der Wissenschaften, Berlin
ARE	J. Breasted, *Ancient Records of Egypt,* Chicago, 1906–1907.
ASAE	*Annales du Service des Antiquités de l'Égypte,* Cairo
ASE	Archaeological Survey of Egypt, London
BdÉ	Bibliothèque d'Étude, Institut Français d'Archéologie Orientale, Cairo
BIÉ	*Bulletin de l'Institut d'Égypte,* Cairo
BIFAO	*Bulletin d'Institut Français d'Archéologie Orientale,* Cairo
CDME	R. O. Faulkner, *Concise Dictionary of Middle Egyptian,* Oxford, 1962
GM	*Göttinger Miszellen,* Göttingen
HÄB	Ägyptolische Beiträge, Hildesheim

IFAO	Institute Français d'Archéologie Orientale, Cairo
JAOS	*Journal of the American Oriental Society,* New Haven
JARCE	*Journal of the American Research Center in Egypt,* New York
JEA	*Journal of Egyptian Archaeology,* London
JEEH	*Journal of European Economic History,* Rome
JEH	*Journal of Economic History,* Wilmington, Del.
JEOL	*Journal Ex Orient Lux,* Leiden
JESHO	*Journal of the Economic and Social History of the Orient,* Leiden
JNES	*Journal of Near Eastern Studies,* Chicago
JSSEA	*Journal of the Society for the Study of Egyptian Antiquities,* Toronto
KRI	K. Kitchen, *Ramesside Inscriptions*
LdÄ	*Lexikon der Ägyptologie*
LD	C. R. Lepsius, *Denkmäler aus Ägypten und Äthiopien,* 12 vols., Berlin, 1849–59
Meir	A. Blackman, *The Rock Tombs of Meir,* 6 vols., London, 1914–53
MIFAO	Memoires publiés par les Membres de l'Institut français d'Archéologie orientale du Caire
MIO	*Mitteilungen des Instituts für Orientforschung,* Berlin
MMA	Metropolitan Museum of Art, New York
MMJ	*Metropolitan Museum Journal,* New York
MMMAFC	*Mémoirs publié par les Membres de la Mission Archéologie Française au Caire,* Paris
PM	B. Porter and R. Moss, *Topographical Bibliography of Ancient Egyptian Hieroglyphic Texts, Reliefs, and Paintings,* Oxford, 1974–present
PT	K. Sethe, *Die Altaegyptischen Pyramidentexte*
REC	*Research in Economic Anthropology,* Greenwich, Conn.
RT	*Recueil de Travaux Rélatifs à la Philologie et à l'Archéologie Égyptiennes et Assyriennes,* Paris
SAK	*Studien zuer Altägyptischen Kultur,* Hamburg
SAOC	Studies in Ancient Oriental Civilization, Chicago
Urk. I	K. Sethe, *Urkunden des Alten Reiches,* Leipzig, 1909

Urk. IV	K. Sethe, *Urkunden der 18. Dynastie,* Leipzig, 1906–1909
Wb.	A. Erman and H. Grapow, *Wörterbuch der Ägyptischen Sprache,* Leipzig, 1926–50
ZÄS	*Zeitschrift für Ägyptische Sprache und Altertumskunde,* Leipzig and Berlin

The Official Gift in Ancient Egypt

Chapter One

The Setting for Exchanges of Inw

Terms and definitions constructed without reference to factual data are hollow; while a mere collecting of facts without a readjustment of our perspective is barren.
Karl Polanyi

The practice of exchanging commodities under the rubric *inw* was known from the earliest periods of Egyptian history. It is attested as early as the time of Ka in the tomb of Horaha.[1] It continues to be known from hieroglyphic inscriptions of Ptolemaic times.[2] Theoretically, at least, it should be possible to trace the history of this term over the course of its continuous use in Egypt for well over three thousand years. Yet the sources for this study do not necessarily allow a simple examination that would yield a complete picture of the development of *inw.*

The accidents of preservation and discovery illuminate certain aspects of *inw* in one period and cast shadow over the same areas in a succeeding era. The examination of *inw* parallels the fable of the wise, blind men who were asked to examine and describe an elephant. Each placed his hand on a different part of the animal's body and described it accurately. Not one, however, could give a consistent overall account of the elephant's appearance. In the same way, the archaeological evidence of the Archaic Period concerning *inw* illustrates that the rubric was used to describe a redistributive economic transaction that always involved the king (see chapter 2). The textual evidence of the New Kingdom suggests that *inw* played an important role in Egypt's foreign relations (see chapter 4). Yet it is clearly not possible to assume a comparable role for *inw* in foreign relations during the Old Kingdom on the basis of this evidence. Unlike the fable of the elephant, it is not certain that the evidence concerning *inw* from different time periods can be combined to yield a complete picture. At least the wise men knew they were all dealing with the same elephant in spite of their differing impressions of it. In the case of *inw* it is not necessarily true or even likely that the word meant exactly the same thing to Ka in the Archaic Period, Ramesses II in the New Kingdom, and the Ptolemies. The problem is to recognize the difference between historical change and the accidents of discovery and preservation.

One solution to this problem is to construct a model of economic transactions in ancient Egypt that can be tested in spite of the different quantities and qualities of evidence available from different periods. The model examined here is based on work originally done for my doctoral dissertation on Egyptian imperialism during the New Kingdom.[3] The model hypothesizes that the Egyptians named economic transactions according to the social status of the participants in the transaction and the institutional setting of the transaction, especially whether the institutions involved were royal or divine. The model was developed from the observation that the same commodity could be exchanged under the rubric *inw* or *b3kw(t)* in the *Annals of Thutmose III.* The only difference between a bull exchanged as *inw* and a bull exchanged as *b3kw(t)* was the personnel involved in the transaction.[4] In the *Annals,* it is clear that *inw* exchanges always occur between the king and another individual. In the case of *b3kw(t)* during the New Kingdom, two institutions, usually a temple and a foreign country, in contrast to the ruler of that country, are the participants in the transaction.[5]

This method of classifying economic transactions stresses the importance of the particular personnel involved and the institutional setting over purely economic considerations. Any approach to the Egyptian economy that assumes the existence of the economic situation known in the modern industrial world cannot accurately describe Egyptian reality. Anthropologists have encountered similar difficulties in understanding and analyzing economic systems throughout the preindustrial world. The following observations are important in considering non-European, preindustrial economic systems.

The first problem for an observer of an ancient or non-European economic transaction is to understand that neither classical capitalist nor Marxist theory applies when the basic institutions of a Western market economy are not present. The economist Nicholas Georgescu-Roegen succinctly describes this situation:

> As soon as we realize that for economic theory an economic system is characterized exclusively by institutional traits, it becomes obvious that neither Marxist nor Standard Theory is valid as a whole for the analysis [of an economy] . . . of which part or all of the capitalist institutions are absent.[6]

The capitalist institutions absent from the ancient Egyptian economy include market mechanisms such as trade for profit or in response to supply and demand and money as a store of value.[7] Karl Polanyi has argued that markets have dominated resource allocation only during the nineteenth century A.D. Otherwise reciprocity and redistribution have controlled allocation and exchange of goods in noncommercial cultures throughout history.

Polanyi begins from the proposition that desire for material gain leads humans to act toward that end, but within the context of a culture. Economists see the human being as an economizing creature. This behavior, however, is a result of conditioning predicated on a market allocation system that forces people to act in a particular manner in order to survive.[8] In non-Western, noncommercial societies, there is at least the possibility of organizing the allocation of resources through redistribution or reciprocity.[9] These allocation methods are often part of the cultural assumptions of people living in non-Western, preindustrial societies. The individual within these societies is conditioned to participate in redistributive activities, although these activities are not necessarily viewed by people within the culture as a means of acquisition. For example, redistribution usually entails an obligation to transfer goods to a political or religious institution. Individuals raised within a culture that stresses the importance of these activities will strive toward this goal. The religious or political institutions then redistribute goods and services on the basis of status within the political or religious realm. Reciprocity requires a transfer of goods on the basis of kinship, friendship, status, or hierarchy.[10] Goods, then, can be allocated within a society to those who need them without an explicit economic motivation. These redistributive or reciprocal activities serve the same structural purpose within a culture as a market does in the West. The people who participated in these activities, however, would not explain their own motivation in terms of profit. These observations allow Polanyi to state,

> Pre-history, early history and indeed . . . the whole of history apart from the last centuries, had economies, the organization of which differed from anything assumed by the economist. And the difference we now begin to infer, can be reduced to a single point—they possessed no system of price-making markets.[11]

Though Polanyi's ideas have been accepted by many Egyptologists,[12] significant objections to his ideas have been raised by economic anthropologists, historians, and some Egyptologists. To a great extent these objections echo the great debates among economic anthropologists of the mid-twentieth century. A general description of these debates will be followed by specific discussion of Polanyi's critics with regard to Egypt.[13]

The critical debates among economic anthropologists in the 1960s and 1970s over how to analyze and understand non-Western economies were between the formalists and the substantivists. Briefly, the debate centered on two types of models that asked different questions about an economy; each party to the debate claimed to stress what was most universal in economies in different cultures, and thus each claimed the more significant results.

The formalist's models were derived from a variety of intellectual traditions, including classical political economy, Marxism, conventional microeconomics, statistics, and marginal utility theory. Marginal utility theory bases its claim to universality on the proposition that resources are scarce everywhere. The economy, in this paradigm, is a system in which individuals rationally calculate how to allocate scarce means among alternative uses. Maximizing an individual's allocation of scarce means is understood by the marginalists to be a universal activity engaged in by all human beings, regardless of cultural context. Simply put, human beings are greedy. The task of the economic historian is then to understand how an individual acts to maximize his or her control over scarce resources. Most formalist models are mathematical and therefore useful in both describing and predicting the actions of "economic man."

The substantivists, on the other hand, have stressed their belief that the most universal attribute of any economy is its organization through institutions. These institutions exist in a specific cultural context; and these institutions, sometimes best understood as process or system, are the unit that should be examined, rather than an individual's actions to maximize access to scarce means. By examining institutions, the substantivists argue, it is possible to examine economic processes across cultures in terms of their similarities and differences. The substantivists give primacy to social relations and emphasize the varieties of arrangements organizing production, distribution, and consumption of resources. This focus sets relationships among different parts of a culture above the actions of an individual. Examples of institutions in this sense are private-property systems, tribute systems, and market systems.

Because of this focus on institutions, the cultural context is critical for the substantivists. Institutions need not be economic in the strict sense to be vital to an understanding of the economy. For example, religious and political considerations are usually essential components of a specific culture's economic institutions. For Polanyi, the originator of substantivism, the relationship of the economy to a society can be highly variable from culture to culture.

Polanyi believed that premarket economies existed in cultures where the economy served societal process, and argued that in premarket economies the economy served to cement social relations. In contrast, market economies suppress social process and make it subservient to the economy. Polanyi's notion of the economy's serving society is basically romantic. In his view there was a time before capitalism and the market when society was primary and the economy served society, rather than vice versa. This was Polanyi's major way of differentiating between premarket and market economies. It is also, probably, the major source of hostility to his ideas. This romanticism, however, should not obscure the major point that Polanyi made, namely that an economy can only be understood in its cultural context.

Polanyi's overriding interest was in the interactions of humans and the organizational principles that regulated people's lives. Polanyi saw that individual activities are meaningful only within a framework. Knowledge of the structure of the whole is essential to understanding the meaning of the behavior of a part. Polanyi's patterns of exchange—reciprocity and redistribution—have meaning only within a particular social, political, and religious context. Therefore, the exchange of birthday gifts among friends in our culture is not true reciprocity. Reciprocal actions of individuals are not enough to establish an economy based on reciprocity and must be distinguished from it. Reciprocity can exist only in a culture where there is little differentiation among classes. Neither is a family's pooling its salaries and having the patriarch dole out allowances truly redistribution. Redistribution occurs only between different social classes and between a geographical center and a periphery. Individual actions are therefore not so important to a general understanding of an economy. Barter does not create a market mode of economic integration. The large structures that keep a society going are the truly important units of analysis.

This emphasis on institutional process and minimizing of individual acts is also a reaction to Adam Smith's "invisible hand." Smith had stated that the acts of self-interested actors trying to maximize individual access to scarce means create an automatic order that we call the market. Polanyi disagreed. For him the market economy is a historically specific system of production, distribution, and consumption. It grew out of specific historical and institutional conditions that cannot be explained by positing univeral psychological traits. Nor can the market be explained by invoking the universal logic of rational action. "For Polanyi," Rhoda Halperin writes, "conventional economic analysis cannot handle the range of institutional arrangements organizing economic processes, because its concepts and assumptions apply only to a market economy."[14]

This is Polanyi's major contribution to economic anthropology, a contribution that was adopted by J. J. Janssen in all of his writings about the ancient Egyptian economy. In Janssen's view, the Egyptian economy was redistributive. All resources moved from the periphery to the center, meaning from individual peasant to the palace or temple, and were redistributed to all on the basis of class and social position. Individual actions of Egyptians have meaning only within this context.

The formalist view of the economy was applied to non-Western cultures by two influential anthropologists, Melville Herskovits and Raymond Firth. Both Herskovits and Firth interpreted the economies of non-Western cultures according to formal economics and the postulate of rational allocation of scarce means. Both scholars used standard theory, believing it to be the only truly scientific approach to the economy. They feared that by abandoning standard theory—that is, formalist and marginal utility theory—they would abandon true scientific inquiry. In his introduction to *Economic Anthropology*, Herskovits began with a discussion of economizing behavior as a universal activity yet admits to some ambivalence in its use:

> In the main, I have tried to follow the conventional categories of economics and *to indicate the points at which economies with which we are concerned diverge so sharply from our own that it is not possible to follow these conventions.*[15]

Raymond Firth demonstrated a similar ambivalence toward standard theory but a dogged determination to use it in the preface to his anthology *Themes in Economic Anthropology*. He directly linked the concept of the formal to economizing behavior and therefore standard theory:

> As will be seen from the various essays, without expressing any very decided specific opinion, the contributions in general imply an acceptance of the view that the logic of scarcity is operative over the whole range of economic phenomena, and that, *however deep and complex may be the influence of social factors, the notions of economy and of economizing are not basically separate.*[16]

Firth argued that the logic of scarcity is operative over the whole range of economic phenomena across all cultures; thus, as long as resources are scarce, economic anthropology is a version of conventional economic science. In spite of this argument, Firth knew that simple societies had economic activities that could not be explained in terms of scarcity or marginality. He knew that scarcity theory was basically ethnocentric because it was derived from only one culture. Both Herskovits and Firth must have realized that they avoided speaking of variation from one culture to the next. Herskovits solved this problem with long descriptive passages, whereas Firth shifted attention from primitive to peasant economies that could more easily be analyzed by standard or formal theory.

Douglas North took another approach to the critique of Polanyi's models.[17] He discerned economizing behavior in the ancient world in the control of transactional costs.[18] Yet he agreed that "all societies have elements of reciprocity, redistribution, and markets in them."[19] North, however, finds "economic motives" behind actions that might be described by a member of the culture in terms of redistribution or reciprocity. Furthermore, he finds that Polanyi's model does not account for change over time.[20]

North is correct that individuals can use a reciprocity system to gain economic advantage. The important point is to consider the methods available within a culture to achieve the fruits of economic advantage: status, an easier life, and prestige. For the Egyptians, all prestige and material goods flowed from the power of the king and the gods. The ability to achieve an easier material life was through service to royal and divine institutions.[21] Even if an analysis of the Egyptian economy is based on Polanyi's somewhat static model, it is still possible to account for change throughout the long course of Egyptian history. It will become clear that the *inw* transaction met the ideal model to a greater and lesser extent based on the power of royal and divine institutions in a particular time period. During periods of diminished central authority, the Egyptians adapted to the real circumstances of their lives. Thus a nomarch might assume the place of the king in the redistributive system during periods of weak or nonexistent central government. When the central government was functioning, however, the model rings true. As North has observed, "Ideology is clearly a critical determinant to understanding the crucial role of government in affecting the costs of exchange in history."[22] Ideology and the culture's belief system play an even more important role in the means of allocating goods and services. Changes in this ideology with changing circumstances will also cause changes in the applicability of Polanyi's model in ancient Egypt.

More detailed critiques of the application of Polanyi's ideas to Egypt are found in the work of Morris Silver and Barry Kemp.[23]

Silver argues that markets did exist along with private merchants in ancient Egypt; Kemp sees the birth of "economic man" in records from ancient Egypt. Both scholars draw on similar evidence. Although Kemp, as an Egyptologist, is more sophisticated in his handling of both textual and archaeological material than Silver, neither scholar convincingly establishes that the ancient Egyptian economy was more closely based on the market model than on the redistributive model.

It is significant that Silver's evidence for private enterprise in ancient Egypt is drawn only from the First Intermediate Period, the very beginning of Dynasty 12, and the end of the Ramesside Period. The activities of Qedes of Gebelein, who was active previous to Dynasty 11; Hekanakht, who was active during the reigns of Amenemhet I or Senwosret I; and the possibly independent agents of *Papyrus Lansing* dating to Dynasty 20 share a background in periods of weak central government. The fact that the redistributive economy did not function in these periods is no surprise. It is perhaps more revealing that no such evidence of the market economy can be adduced from any reign of the Old, Middle, or New Kingdoms. It seems clear that the redistributive economy is the only one that can be studied during periods of strong central government, inasmuch as it is the only one that left any evidence.

Silver introduces Berlin Stela 24032 as evidence that ancient Egyptian individuals owned granaries and boats. This stela belonged to a Nubian mercenary named Qedes, who lived in the time immediately preceding Dynasty 11.[24] In this short inscription, Qedes summarizes his lifetime achievements, which include the acquisition of oxen and goats, granaries filled with Upper Egyptian wheat, and a small boat of thirty cubits, which he used as a ferry during the inundation. This sort of activity hardly establishes a market economy. The granaries in question are represented in the inscription by a sign that Henry G. Fischer read *mẖr* or *mḥr*.[25] Fischer points out that this type of granary is a storage bin.[26] Thus it cannot be the basis for a grain merchant's business. Qedes claims only ownership of a storage facility, probably meaning that he was not totally dependent on the communal granaries known throughout Egypt.[27] He never mentions selling or even bartering with the grain. Ownership of a ferry boat shows some initiative, clearly, but cannot be understood as part of a widespread labor market or service industry. There is no reason to believe that Qedes's accomplishments establish the existence of market exchange. But Qedes may illustrate the sort of person Ipuwer described as, "he who had not grain is (now) the owner of granaries."[28] Ipuwer expressed alarm over this situation because it was so far from the Egyptian ideal.

The stela of Qedes illustrates that the First Intermediate Period witnessed a breakdown in the economic norm parallel to the other changes in political and religious life in this period. Yet local headman redistribution was present in Qedes's time. He was a contemporary of Ankhtyfy, who filled the vacuum created by the lack of central government by his redistributive activities, as we will see.

Hekanakht's papers point to a much more complicated issue: the status of land ownership in ancient Egypt in different periods. Living at the beginning of Dynasty Twelve, Hekanakht clearly engaged in the rental of land and loaning of grain.[29] Baer emphasizes that private land rental was widespread in all periods. This is of course significant, but there can be little doubt that this land was reckoned as integral to the redistributive economy during periods of strong central government. It is unknown whether people like Hekanakht survived the governmental reforms of Senwosret III. Much of the rentable land during the New Kingdom was leased from temples.[30] This hardly constituted a market in land independent of the redistributive economy.

Silver refers to a number of textual sources to establish his belief that there were private merchants in ancient Egypt. He establishes this point by asserting that there were merchants who were subject to tax collection and therefore not government employees.[31] He first quotes Aylward M. Blackman and T. Eric Peet's translation of *P. Lansing* 4:8–10.[32] It reads,

> (4:8) The merchants (*šwty*) fare downstream and upstream (4:9) and are busy as can be, carrying wares ⟨from⟩ one town to another, and supplying him that hath not, But the tax-gatherers (4:10) exact(?) gold, the most precious of all minerals.[33]

The crucial line for establishing taxation of the "merchants" is 4:9, "But the tax-gatherers exact (?) gold." The verb that Blackman and Peet query is *f3i,* and the meaning of this verb is the key to whether or not "merchants" are "taxed."

Two points might be raised against this theory. First, *f3i* is more likely correctly translated here as "to carry," just as the very same verb is translated in the preceding line, "The merchants fare downstream . . . carrying wares." Both Faulkner and the *Wörterbuch* translate *f3i* as "carry," though Faulkner also gives the specialized sense of "deliver" when used with "taxes."[34]

Furthermore, even if the tax-collectors were exacting gold, the text does not specify that it is exacted from the "merchants." The passage seems to be describing two types of Nile traffic: the "merchants" and the tax-collectors, each performing their duties. There is no reason to believe that the "merchants" are the object of the tax-collectors' activities.

It is even less understandable that Blackman and Peet translate *f3i* in line 4:10 as "exact" when the same word is used with "merchants" as its subject in line 4:9.[35] Rather than suggesting that these "merchants" are taxed, the author of *P. Lansing,* while describing the disadvantages of all occupations other than that of scribe, is pointing out that truly valuable cargoes are not handled by the "merchants," not that they are taxed.

A second source referred to by Silver to prove the taxation of shipping and thus the existence of independent, private merchants is the Nauri Decree of Sety I. Silver seems to have misunderstood the purpose of the decree. In his publication of the Nauri Decree, F. Ll. Griffith observes, "The purpose of the decree is to safeguard the rights of a great royal foundation, and of all individuals and property connected to it."[36] The inscription states that the foundation, called the "House of Millions of Years of the King of Upper and Lower Egypt Menmaatre (Sety I) 'Heart at

Ease in Abydos' " was created by the king. The boats that are protected from interference are those that Sety I himself gave to the temple.[37] These boats are exempted from any interference by the vizier, officers and courtiers, the judicial council, the viceroy of Kush, the chiefs of foreign contingents, superintendents of gold, mayors, controllers of camps, and so on—all royal appointees. The decree goes on to state, "His Majesty has commanded . . . to prevent any interference with any person belonging to the House [of Millions of Years, etc.] . . . to prevent their boat being stopped on water by any patrol."[38] The king is merely ensuring that the personnel and equipment that he provided to this temple are used for the intended purpose and are not diverted by local royal officials to other purposes. The decree's value for determining whether "private merchants" are taxed is nil.

Another proof Silver adduces for taxation of shipping by private merchants is the statement that "Nectanebo I granted the temple of Neith one-tenth of the royal taxes collected on seaborne imports to Naucratis."[39] This evidence is irrelevant to a discussion of the ancient Egyptian economy before the foundation of Naucratis. This is a very special case where the Egyptians had entered into trade with the Hellenistic Greeks, who had used money as a store of value for centuries by the time of Nectanebo I. By Dynasty 30, the Egyptians were issuing coinage.[40] Thus the Egyptian economy had changed significantly from its classical phase.

Further evidence for merchants in Egypt is adduced by Silver from *Papyrus Sallier* II, a text known to Egyptologists as the "Satire on the Trades." He quotes the following translation of line 5:5–6. "The itinerant merchant sails downstream to the Delta to get trade for himself. When he has done more than his arms can (really) do, the gnats have slain him, the sand flies have made him miserably miserable. Then there is inflammation."[41] Yet Silver is not aware of the numerous difficulties in this text and with this translation. The word translated as "itinerant merchant" is *bty*, a word whose meaning has been discussed by Brunner and Helck.[42]

First, other attestations of the word *bty* indicate that he is not free of institutional ties. An example from a sarcophagus found in a Theban tomb refers to the *imy-r bty n Imn,* "the overseer of the *bty* of Amun."[43] Louvre Stela 421 knows an *imy-r bty,* even though it omits the name of the institution. However, both titles indicate that the *bty* works within an institutional setting. Second, Brunner remarks that the nature of the *bty*'s difficulty is physical. He works too hard with his arms and is attacked by natural pests. This would not be the expected problem for a merchant. Brunner suggests that what is intended here is *bty,* a shepherd—a profession associated with the Delta. The nearly homophonic *bty* is known from the Tombs of Ti and of Mereruka. Thus Brunner sees *bty* as a false archaism.[44]

The best solution to the problem is surely that offered by Helck, to read *biti* with the parallel text GC 81,9. This would yield, "The reed worker travels to the Delta to haul arrows." Thus the connection with merchants is entirely broken.[45]

Silver also makes reference to a document of Ramesses II in which temples turned over goods to merchants for sale in markets. This is an apparent reference to the Great Dedicatory Inscription of Abydos.[46] Here again it is a question of the *šwty,* here spelled *šwyt,* probably a temple agent. Ramesses II has clearly assigned the people referred to by this title to Sety I's temple in Abydos. Ramesses then promises, "The š*wyt* do š*wyt*-activity bearing their purpose (?) and their temple dues thereof consisting of gold and copper."[47] Again, in spite of some difficulties with the meanings of various words, this inscription is dealing with agents of the temple working within an institutional setting.[48]

Silver also discusses the evidence of *P. Louvre* E3226. He states that this papyrus, an administrative document from a granary,

> shows that departments of the royal administration regularly gave grain to specialised traders (*bnryw*) who, somewhat later, delivered dates. The terminology employed raises the possibility that the grain was sold and the proceeds used to purchase dates, or perhaps this was a barter transaction. The document does not disclose who produced

> the dates or where they originated. On the other hand, it is apparent that the date sellers were not government employees.[49]

A closer reading of the actual text might revise this opinion. Silver is apparently referring to A recto vii and viii and A verso vii and viii. These *bnryw* were given grain, a fact that is clear from the use of the verb *rdi.* As will be shown below, this verb should not be translated "sold," but only "gave." They, however, do not return dates, *bnryt,* but rather in all cases return to the granary *bnrt,* "date-cakes."[50] Indeed these people, whose title should be transliterated *bnrytyw,* are probably manufacturing cakes from the grain and dates, which are then returned to the granary. They are not merchants at all, but, as Faulkner translates, "confectioners."[51] In both A recto vii and A verso vii, the *bnrytyw* in question are identified as *nty r-ḫt sš Ḥpw n imy-r šnwty Mnw-Nḫt,* "those who are under the authority of the scribe Hepu of the Overseer of the Granary, Min-Nakht."[52] It is true that it cannot be determined whether or not the granary of which Min-Nakht is overseer is owned by the king. But such a title is certainly an indication that the *bnryty* is attached to an institution and not a free agent. However, this passage can be used only to show that date cakes were not baked on the premises of the granary in this particular case.

Silver also adduces private ownership of boats as evidence for private traders.[53] Proof is deduced from Berlin Stela 24032 (Qedes of Gebelein already discussed above), the Edict of Horemheb, *P. Anastasi* IV, and *P. Amiens.* The Edict of Horemheb does seem to refer to the private ownership of boats. Yet nowhere does it mention that privately owned boats are used for trade. Indeed, the references to private boats most often refer to situations in which they are used to deliver offerings to the royal harim[54] or to do some royal service.[55]

Silver uses *P. Anastasi* IV 3:10 to show that "even a seagoing vessel was not beyond the means of a rich man."[56] The sentence in question reads, "Your ship is come from Khor loaded with all manner of good things."[57] The context of this sentence is advice on the benefits of serving Amun. The introduction to this document notes, "Let your heart be set upon pleasing Amun . . . that you may spend a lifetime of happiness until you reach beatitude."[58] Ownership of a ship loaded with Syrian merchandise is one of those benefits. However, there is no hint in the text that this merchandise is then to be sold. Thus even private ship ownership in this context does not provide proof of private trade for profit.

The names of ships are another proof used by Silver to show that ships were privately owned. Silver quotes Torgny Säve-Söderbergh to the effect that the format for ship names in Egyptian was "Ship of PN."[59] Säve-Söderbergh's examples are drawn from *P. Louvre* 3171, also known as *P. Amiens*. Indeed the initial part of the naming formula for ships in this papyrus show examples such as "Ship of the Captain Ashafemhab son of Neferronpe."[60] The name, however, continues, "of the House of Amun." Alan H. Gardiner, in fact, commented on the actual ownership of these ships in the initial publication of *P.Amiens*:

> Of the twenty-one ships united in this same expedition [described in *P. Amiens*] the names of the captains are preserved in only eight cases. *That the ships themselves belonged to the great temple of Amun is plain from the words "of the House of Amen-Re King of the Gods" in one case (3;13) and from the shorter description "of the house of Amen" (I 1:9; 2:4; 3:4) or "of this House" (2:10; 4:4,9) in the rest.*[61]

Clearly, these passages do not support the idea of private ship ownership in ancient Egypt. These ships were temple property. Individual ships are designated by the captain's name in order to differentiate them in the records. Private shipping did exist during the later Ramesside Period and in the first millennium, but is less well documented in periods of strong central government.[62]

The word *pr*, meaning "commercial firm," is also adduced by Silver as proof of private trading in ancient Egypt. He cites *P. Lansing* 4:10 once again to support this point.[63] Similar attempts to associate *pr* with a commercial establishment are found in Ricardo Caminos's translation of *P. Lansing*, in Peet's translation of the Tomb Robbery papyri, and in Edward Wente's translation of

Wenamun 2:1.[64] Helck, however, has shown that this translation is unlikely except possibly in the case of Wenamun. *pr* can mean either "house" or "temple." Used alone it can refer to either a private household of a person, or the "household" of a god. However, it cannot be used with the meaning "commercial house." This is clear in *P.B.M.* 10068, where the *pr-Sbk,* Temple of Sobek, is tabulated next to the *tu-hi-r* Chiefs or the Chantress of Sobek.[65] Helck also doubts Silver's other example of a commercial house from Wenamun 2:1. The passage reads, "As for . . . Sidon . . . surely there are . . . fifty freighters there which are in commerce with Warkatara, for it is to his 'house' that they haul."[66] As Helck points out, it is perfectly possible that *pr* in this case refers to the actual building that houses Warkatara's business.[67] Even if the Egyptian here is trying to convey the sense of "commercial house," two points must be made. First, this business is located outside of Egypt and as such could not be considered to be part of the general Egyptian economy. Second, the circumstances of Dynasty 21 reflected here, a time of weak kings and divided rule, cannot be read back to the heights of Egyptian power during the New Kingdom.

In sum, the evidence Silver adduces does not negate the fact that there is almost no conclusive evidence for private merchants in ancient Egypt. His argument is based either on outdated translations of texts that can now be improved or on statements removed from their context. Many of the examples come from periods of weak central government, the periods when reality did not fit the model of royal domination of resource allocation. These examples cannot be used to establish the nature of the Egyptian allocation system during periods of strong centralized political power.

Barry Kemp also offers a critique of the redistributive model of the ancient Egyptian economy.[68] On the most basic level, by removing individual phenomena from their cultural and even historical context, Kemp's arguments about individual actions of specific Egyptians make them seem amenable to analysis by standard economic theory. If these actions are viewed through the specific context of Egypt's economy, they take on a different meaning.

Kemp objects to the exclusive characterization of any economy as purely market-driven or purely redistributive; no one system can meet all human needs.[69] This statement is in fact a direct reference to marginal utility theory: that the proper study of the economy is the study of rational allocation of scarce means and maximizing activities on the part of individuals. Kemp examines how the system failed to keep its promise to support people who participated in it.

To answer this question he concentrates on the First Intermediate Period to examine economic conditions in the absence of a central government. He finds that tombs in Qau and Badari, dating to Dynasties 7/8, contain grave goods of higher value and quality than local tombs dating to the Old Kingdom.[70] The absence of a central government apparently led to greater prosperity at the local level. The best resources could remain at home rather than be collected by the central government.

The archive of Hekanakht, letters written by a farmer at the end of Dynasty 11 or beginning of Dynasty 12, also illustrates conditions without a strong central government.[71] In his letters, there is clear evidence that Hekanakht loaned grain at interest, paid rent on land in advance, and had a "capital" in copper, oil, and cloth. Hekanakht is an excellent example of a person operating at a time when there was not yet a firmly established central government. His archive demonstrates that the ancient Egyptians were capable of looking after themselves when the government did not interfere.

But a second kind of response to the lack of central government is found in Ankhtyfy's tomb biography, which also dates to the First Intermediate Period.[72] This biography reveals the more common impulse of an ancient Egyptian potentate in the absence of central government: to claim for himself the privileges formerly reserved for the king. After conquering the neighboring nomes, Ankhtyfy distributed famine relief, surely in return for the promise that he would now be the central authority that collected from the next successful harvest. The redistributive economy was reestablished on a smaller scale.

Kemp introduces other evidence for aspects of the economy not under the control of the central authority during the major periods of central government. But it is less convincing than the evidence he adduces from the First Intermediate Period. From the Old Kingdom, Kemp refers to the "shops" or market found in tomb reliefs of Dynasties 5, 6 and 18.[73] Here barter of the type attested by Deir el Medinah ostraca is depicted on the river bank. People exchange one food product for another and home furnishings such as vessels in an effort to vary their diets and have access to other people's skills in making specific objects. These scenes, as Kemp would agree, will support either the redistributive hypothesis or will supply evidence for a market economy. The actual position of the shopkeepers—independent or representatives of the temple—is nowhere indicated in the reliefs. These scenes will fit whatever preconceptions one brings to them.

Kemp introduces the scene from the tomb of Khnumhotep II at Beni Hasan depicting Levantine tribesmen delivering eyepaint to demonstrate local independence from the central authority.[74] He uses this scene to show that foreigners had direct contact with nomarchs and could bypass the king. However, a careful examination of the scene will show that these tribesmen are introduced to Khnumhotep by a small figure labeled as the royal document scribe Neferhotep.[75] This scene of diplomatic gift-giving shows Khnumhotep receiving a gift from the King or at least demonstrating such activities were under token royal control.

In the New Kingdom, Kemp adduces the differing sizes of Amarna houses, the Amarna gold hoard, and the *šwty* as evidence for a market-driven economy during a period of strong central government. Here his argument is much less compelling if these individual actions are placed in their historical and cultural context.

A hoard of gold was discovered in Amarna by Henri Frankfort and J. D. S. Pendlebury.[76] Known as the el-Till hoard, it weighed over three thousand grams, taking the form of bars and roughly made rings. There was also a silver figurine and other rough scraps of silver included, weighing over one thousand grams.[77] The hoard has been interpreted as a thief's loot or a jeweler's stock. Kemp believes, whatever its origin, "it illustrates easily convertible wealth poised on the point of re-entering the economy at a private level."[78] But even if this is true, the method by which this wealth reenters the economy is not self-evident from the bars of gold. Only the royal government could be expected to acquire bars of gold. In any case, Amarna was the quintessential government town. Only government officials and those who served them lived there.

The fact that Amarna was a government town must also be kept in mind when observing varying house sizes at Amarna. This is Kemp's evidence of an interest in status, wealth, and power, and therefore an interest in acquisition. Polanyi's romanticism perhaps ignores human greed, but this is not a necessary component of using his models. Placing actions in a cultural context means recognizing that the route to satisfying greed varies from culture to culture. In Egypt, the quickest route to status, wealth, and power is royal favor. It is hard to believe that anyone living in Amarna received his house as a result of anything other than the king's pleasure. Naturally, higher officials received better, larger houses.

Finally, Kemp examines the issue of the *šwty*, translated by some as merchants, but easily understood as temple agent in almost all contexts in which it is found in Egyptian texts. The *šwty* is also the major receiver of stolen goods in the Tomb Robbery papyrus. This significant illegal activity on the part of the *šwty* is also a part of the economy, as Kemp has shown. This is an important observation. However, it is more important to remember that the *šwty* is outside the social system when he acts illegally. It is doubtful that his role could have been very important in the overall economic life of Egypt. Not one written document attributed to a *šwty* is known to have survived from ancient Egypt. Writing was invented to keep track of economic transactions. Why, if private trading had any real significance, is it so difficult to locate in the ancient record?

In conclusion, Kemp's use of marginal utility theory in the formalist tradition to understand specific behaviors in the record from ancient Egypt does not present a fair picture of the economy. These individual activities have more or less significance depending on the strength of the central government. Even during periods of strong government the occasional evidence of activities outside its control are less economically significant. Despite Polanyi's romanticism, it is clearly possible to use his redistributive model to gain the clearest picture of ancient Egypt's economy.

The Egyptians actually lacked a vocabulary for the concepts of buying, selling, and money. They did use otherwise common words such as *ini,* "to bring, to acquire," and *rdi,* "to give," to describe their barter. Peet's attempt to associate *ini* with "to buy" and *rdi* with "to sell" founders on the very examples he quotes in support of the argument. As Peet himself points out, "Egyptian phraseology makes no distinction of kind between a commodity and an amount of silver or copper exchanged for it. . . . The Egyptian though he possessed the conception of money as 'exchange metal' still clung to the language of barter."[79] For example, a passage in *P.B.M.* 10052 8:6–7, says, "I gave (*rdit*) some barley to the workman Pnufer and he gave (*rdit*) me 2 kite of silver." Here, no distinction is made between buying and selling because these exchanges of commodities are seen as barter. Peet's identification of *rdit* with the English "to sell" would mean that both parties to this agreement would be selling rather than one buying and the other selling. In fact, the Egyptians of the Ramesside Period most commonly used the verbs *ini,* "to bring, to acquire," or *rdi,* "to give," followed by *ḥr, r isw,* or *r ḏb3,* all of which could be understood as "in exchange for." The psychological difference between buying and selling is not recognized if the actions of both parties in a transaction are described with the same verb. A true profitmaking exchange would have to recognize this essential difference between buying and selling.

So-called long-distance trade in ancient Egypt, the "royal monopoly," also demonstrates that a clear distinction must be made between commodity exchanges based on a market mechanism or trade for profit and merely the commissioned importation of goods through barter. In forming this distinction, the market mechanism for price-setting and trade for profit must be understood to mean consciously buying cheap in order to sell dear. Ancient Egyptian long-distance trade exhibits a distinct lack of interest in or understanding of this concept.

One of the earliest "trading" expeditions known through Egyptian sources is that of Harkhuf.[80] His tomb biography makes it clear that his motivation for going on the trip to Nubia was to bring back goods ordered by the king.[81] Though financial gain most probably resulted from the king's praise, Harkhuf emphasizes that this was his major reward, not financial profit.

An even clearer distinction between true long-distance trade for profit and the Egyptian commissioned expedition can be found in Wadi Hammamat Inscription No. 192. Here King Mentuhotep IV emphasizes his explicit command to his official Amenemhet (the future Amenemhet I), "to bring me a precious block of pure stone from this mountain."[82] This expedition could only be considered true trade for profit if it were part of an at least semiregular quarrying trip made to import stone into Egypt regardless of whether the ultimate destination of the stone was known in advance. True trade would require the expedition leader to import stone, which would cost him a specific amount for labor, travel expenses, and so on, and then to sell the stone for more than his costs. There is no clear example of merchants in this sense in ancient Egypt. Yet there are many examples of what might be called commissioned trade in Egypt.

A New Kingdom example of such commissioned trade would be the expedition that Hatshepsut sent to Punt in order to bring back incense for the Temple of Amun.[83] Here the expedition was conceived as a fulfillment of an oracle which Hatshepsut received from the god, Amun. Hatshepsut sent an expedition with explicit instructions to bring back incense for the specific use of the temple. The incense was brought in the form of trees to be transplanted at the temple. This trade entailed no risk and no profit. It provided a commodity that was desired and for which the use was known in advance.

The *Report of Wenamun* is another source for ancient Egyptian trade.[84] The heading describes the report in the following terms:

> Year 5, fourth month of summer, day 16, the day of departure of Wenamun, the Elder of the Portal of the Temple of Amun, Lord of Thrones-of-the-Two-Lands, to fetch timber for the great noble bark of Amen-Re, King of the Gods, which is upon the river and [is called] Amen-user-re.[85]

This passage also explicates the Egyptian view of long-distance trade. An official of the Temple of Amen-Re made the trip to Lebanon to buy a specific amount of wood for a specific purpose. There was never any consideration of buying extra wood that might be sold at a profit on the return to Egypt. The trade was commissioned by the temple only to fill an order for known needs. Any element of business risk is completely missing from Egyptian records of trade. The Egyptian trader filled orders only for the institutional structure to which he was attached. Egyptian expedition leaders functioned more as organizers who directed the personnel who fetch and deliver goods rather than traders who took a business risk in hopes of realizing a profit.

This lack of interest in the profit motive probably stemmed from the complete lack of true money in the ancient Egyptian economy. Coinage was unknown to the Egyptians before Dynasty 26.[86] It was not actually issued by Egyptian kings until Dynasty 29, and only came into common use with the arrival of Alexander the Great in Egypt.[87] There is, of course, a distinction between coinage and money.[88] Money lies behind coinage and can act as a medium of exchange, a standard of value, or a store of value.[89] Though the Egyptians did occasionally use gold, silver, and copper as a medium of exchange and more often as a standard of value, they did not actually acquire precious metal in order to build up wealth, that is, establish it as a store of value. As James W. Curtis has observed,

> the prime requisites for the development of money and coinage were missing in Ancient Egypt. The lack of private enterprise, the homogeneity of the economic structure and of productive efforts, the relative geographic isolation, the royal monopoly of trade, and the marginal economic status of the millions of fellahin who formed the great bulk of the population were all negative factors.[90]

Clearly, the Egyptians understood the concept of precious metals used as a standard of value in order to facilitate barter. Gardiner and Jaroslav Černý have each discussed a contract dating to Year 15 of Ramesses II that proves this use of precious metal.[91] A certain Erenofre desired to acquire a slave girl valued at 4 deben, 1 kite of silver. She offered textiles worth 2 deben, 2.33 kite, bronze vessels, a pot of honey, ten shirts, and 10 deben of copper in return for her. These commodities equaled the value of 4 deben, 1 kite of silver. In a second example published by Černý, an ox valued at 120 deben of copper was exchanged for two pots of fat (60 deben), five shirts (25 deben), one dress (20 deben), and one hide (15 deben), equaling 120 deben, the value of the ox.

In a barter system such as this, there is no way to achieve a profit through selling. Goods are acquired because a person or institution has a need for them. There is no capital formation; there is no investment in order to increase an individual's wealth.

If the Egyptians could not amass capital as wealth through trade for profit and money, there had to be other forces that motivated the economy. George Dalton has argued that preindustrial economies do not actually recognize the economy as a separate structure within society. On the basis of a comparison of a large number of nonmarket economies, he has stated,

> A distinguishing characteristic of . . . [premarket economic life] is the fusion of social and economic institutions. Indeed even "fusion" is distorting because it implies the bringing together of separate elements. It would be better to say that there is no awareness of the "economy" as a distinct set of practises apart from social institutions.

> Transactions of material goods in marketless economies are expressive of social obligations which have neither mechanism nor meaning of their own apart from social ties, social obligations, and social situations [that] they express. In the Western meaning of the word, there is no "economy" in traditional society; only socio-economic institutions, processes, and transactions.[92]

In Dalton's analysis, which is based on the work of Karl Polanyi, economic transactions cement social relationships as well as reallocate goods where they are needed. The social structure provides motivation for economic actions. Men attain prestige when they earn the king's praise for bringing an expedition to a successful conclusion. The king also rewards his loyal followers with tomb equipment (see chapter 2) as well as goods in this life.

This view of the economic system suggests that a study of the ancient economy is dependent on an understanding of the political, religious, social, and psychological situation more than purely economic considerations. Therefore, the main focus of the following pages will be to examine *inw* from its earliest examples through the New Kingdom as an economic transaction embedded in a economy that is totally fused within the social system.

Egypt was a society that in fact did not distinguish the economy as an entity separate from other social institutions. Disregard of this basic concept has led scholars to translate the word *inw* by thirty-eight different words in English, French, and German.[93] The Egyptians could not have been as vague as the numerous translations suggest. They must have seen an underlying unity in transactions called *inw*. This unity is found in the fact that transactions involving *inw* always include the king as either giver or receiver of the goods. Thus the focus of the analysis of *inw* will be on the participants in the transaction and the institutional setting in which it took place. In contrast, other rubrics used by the Egyptians to describe economic transactions involve other persons or institutions. This study will show that *inw* is a transaction that expresses a socioeconomic relationship between the king and others. Commodities exchanged under the rubric *inw* are goods that are either entering or leaving the king's privy-purse and are comparable to gifts in other cultures.

Finally, this study rests on the assumption that distinctions made by the ancient Egyptians in different rubrics to describe economic transactions are meaningful and consistent, even if their inner logic is not always clear to modern historians. The task is to understand the Egyptian economy on its own terms, rather than impose a modern set of criteria on the evidence.

Chapter Two

The Emergence and Development of Inw *Exchanges during the Archaic Period and the Old Kingdom*

From the very beginning, transactions that the Egyptians described as *inw* involved the king as one of the participants in the exchange. This fact has been obscured by the difficulties of transcribing and understanding the laconic texts attesting *inw* from the earliest period. *Inw* was part of the royal redistribution of products to members of the royal family, the bureaucrats who directly served the king, and even lower officials. A close examination of the archaeological contexts of inscriptions containing the rubric reveals that some gifts from the king to others were called *inw* by the Egyptians. These characteristics of *inw* exchanges are fully recognizable in the archaeological and historical records by Dynasty 1. By Dynasties 5 and 6 there is enough evidence to construct an even clearer picture of exchanges of *inw*.

Dynasty 1

Examples of *inw* attested from Dynasty 1 consist of ten labels and tags made of ivory or ebony, perhaps originally attached to containers, and seals and ink inscriptions on jars. These labels include the type Peter Kaplony calls a "*Steuer-vermerke*" or tax-notations.[1] They were discovered in mastabahs located in Nagada, Abydos, and Saqqara. The word was written with the bulti-fish and the *nw*-jar, . Very often the sedge-plant preceded this group, .[2] In later periods the bulti-fish had the phonetic value *in* in the writing of words such as *int,* "valley," or *inb,* "wall." The *nw*-jar already had its known value. The sign that appears ambiguous to modern readers in value is the sedge-plant. If it can be determined that the correct value of this sign was always *nsw,* "King of Upper Egypt," in this phrase, rather than *šm*^{c}*w,* "Upper Egypt," the argument that *inw* was always explicitly described as property of the king by the Egyptians in this period can be made.

In Egyptian writing of Dynasty 1, no distinction was made between M.23, the sedge-plant, and M.24, the flowering sedge-plant, . Kaplony remarks, "The two signs were not differentiated on offering texts."[3] Kaplony found it difficult in some cases to decide which word was intended in a particular label or sealing. For example, on a sealing from Saqqara Tomb 3357, Kaplony translated "Royal Palace or Upper Egyptian Palace."[4] Yet in other cases he preferred one reading over another. When the sedge-plant was combined with the bee, (G.S.L. L.2) for *bity,* "King of Lower Egypt," the sedge-plant surely must have been read *nsw,* "King of Upper Egypt."[5] But another criterion can also help in determining whether the sedge-plant's phonetic value was intended to be *nsw* or *šm*^{c}*w,* honorific transposition. This is the Egyptian convention of writing signs that mean either "king" and its derivatives or "god" and its derivatives first in set phrases. These groups therefore were not written in the same order in which they were pronounced. The name was derived from the idea that the Egyptians honored the words for "king" or "god" in these writings.

Honorific transposition was used in Egyptian inscriptions as early as the Narmer Palette. Here the name of the sandal bearer was written with the rosette having the phonetic value *nsw*, "royal." The rosette was written before the *ḥm*-sign in honorific transposition.[6] *Inw* notations depicted the sedge-plant first. Kaplony, who read these signs as *šm*^{c}*w*, "Upper Egypt" observes, "The name of the province is written . . . before or above the name of the tax. Upper Egypt is written accurately or hastily like *nsw*."[7] Yet there is no grammatical way to render signs arranged in the common manner used in these inscriptions "*inw* of Upper Egypt." If, however, the sedge-plant's value were *nsw*, there is no problem in understanding the arrangement of the text. *Nsw* was written in honorific transposition yielding "*inw* of the King of Upper Egypt."

One problem remains before accepting this solution. The signs for *inw* could be combined with the clump of papyrus (G.S.L. M.16), , understood by Kaplony as *mḥw*, "Lower Egypt." The clump of papyrus also was always written before or above the word for *inw* in these early documents. This apparent anomaly can be solved by reference to Junker's suggestion that the clump of papyrus had the phonetic value *bity*, "King of Upper Egypt," in the early period.[8] Thus in the case where the clump of papyrus was written before *inw*, the grammatical difficulty also can be resolved. Here the clump of papyrus had the phonetic value *bity*, "King of Lower Egypt," written in honorific transposition. The proper rendering would then be, "*inw* of the King of Lower Egypt."

These two improvements in readings of the texts reveal that the king was always one of the participants in exchanges of *inw*. Two methods can be used to prove that *inw* was exchanged only between the king and others. First, inscriptional evidence shows that *inw* was always mentioned in a context that named the king either as the donor or recipient of commodities marked *inw*. Second, archaeological context demonstrates that *inw* was found in the tombs of kings, royal retainers, and even one commoner during this period. Therefore, the king used it for his own purposes, including redistribution. The following examples demonstrate that the king was always a participant in the exchange of *inw*.

Inw *Found in Royal Archaeological Contexts*

1. *sṯi-Ḥr 400 inw Ḥr nsw bity*
   Sṯi-ḥr-oil 400: the *inw* of the Horus and King of Upper and Lower Egypt.
   Dyn. 1, Djer[9]
   Context: Tomb of Djer, Abydos.

2. *inw nsw bity*
   Inw of the King of Upper and Lower Egypt.
   Dyn. 1, De(we)n[10]
   Context: Tomb of De(we)n, Abydos.

According to the preponderance of scholarly opinion today, the king's tombs of Dynasties 1 and 2 were located at Abydos.[11] Once this fact is taken into account, only two examples of commodities marked as *inw* found in the king's possession during Dynasty 1 have been discovered. This paucity of material is clearly the result of the peculiar excavation history of the royal tombs at Abydos.[12] Émile C. Amélineau's purposeful destruction of valuable historical evidence in order to increase the monetary value of the surviving objects was most likely responsible for this small sample. Thus there can be no statistical significance to the small number of *inw*-commodities retained by the king during Dynasty 1 in the surviving record.

Inw *in Tombs Not Assigned to Kings*

The following examples of *inw* were found in tombs now believed to belong to members of the royal family, high officials, and a commoner.

3. *ḏf(3) nsw . . . inw nsw*
   Provisions of the King of Upper Egypt and the *inw* of the King of Upper Egypt.

Dyn. 1, Aha[13]
Context: Tomb of Rekhyt, Nagada

4. *Ḥr ᶜḥ3 mri . . . inw nsw*
The Horus Aha, *mri*-oil . . . the *inw* of the King of Upper Egypt.
Dyn. 1, Aha[14]
Context: Tomb of a high official, Tomb 3357, Saqqara.

5. *ẖt 1100 in(w) nsw*
H̱t-oil 1100; *in(w)* of the King of Upper Egypt.
Dyn. 1, Wadji[15]
Context: Tomb of the high official Sekhemka, Tomb 3504 at Saqqara.

6. *ẖt 1100 [inw] nsw*
H̱t-oil 1100: [*inw*] of the King of Lower Egypt.
Dyn. 1, Wadji[16]
Context: Assigned to the tomb of the high official Sekhemka, Tomb 3504 at Saqqara.

7. *Ḥr Dwn sṯi inw bity*
The Horus Den, *sṯi*-oil, *inw* of the King of Lower Egypt.
Dyn. 1, De(we)n[17]
Context: Tomb of Queen Her-neith, Tomb 3507 at Saqqara.

8. *inw nsw S3k3*
Inw of the King of Upper Egypt, Saka.
Dyn. 1, De(we)n[18]
Context: Tomb of Queen Meret-Neith, Abydos.

9. *Sṯi-ḥr 600 inw nsw Šmᶜw*
Sṯi-ḥr oil 600: *inw* of the King of Upper Egypt and (from?) Upper Egypt.
Dyn. 1, De(we)n[19]

Context: Tomb of Hemaka, Tomb 3035 at Saqqara.

10. *Dwn inw nsw*
    Den: *inw* of the King of Upper Egypt.
    Dyn. 1, De(we)n[20]
    Context: Tomb 230, Middle Class Cemetery west of Tomb of Ti, Saqqara.

Redistribution of commodities marked *inw* is attested for the reigns of Aha, Wadji, and De(we)n during the First Dynasty. A wide variety of people received *inw* from these kings. In fact, it is possible to argue that the system or rules by which *inw* was redistributed was fully in place at this early date.

Members of the royal family are represented by queens Herneith and Meret-neith. They both received *inw* from De(we)n. This find anticipates more fully documented transfers of *inw* to queens in Dynasty 13.[21]

High officials of the central government in Memphis also received *inw* for their tombs. This is clear from finds in Saqqara tombs 3035, 3357, and 3504. In fact, examples of *inw* in these tombs point to the practice of rewarding high officials with *inw* as early as the first reign of Dynasty 1. Petty officials also received *inw* from the king as early as the time of De(we)n as at Tomb 230 in Saqqara.

The example of *inw* that comes from the so-called "Tomb of Mena" at Nagada, probably belonging to the local prince Rekhyt, demonstrates that Aha also rewarded local rulers with *inw*. This foreshadows similar transfers to local rulers in the Middle Kingdom.

Even with the scanty evidence preserved today, it is clear that the redistribution of *inw* was an established practice by the very beginning of Dynasty 1. This fact suggests that the practice originated in prehistory at a time when Egypt was more accurately described as a chiefdom than a true state. To some extent this observation allays the discomfort felt by some scholars in applying to Egypt a model derived largely from cultures and societies that were less politically complex. As Ann Macy Roth has observed in another context, historic Egyptian society and cultural institutions developed smoothly and without interruption from predynastic ancestors.[22] The practice of redistributing commodities under the rubric *inw* must have been one of the ancient customs that survived into and developed through historic times.

Dynasty 2

By the Second Dynasty, the word *inw* was written with the *nw*-jar combined with walking legs, , the form the word took for the next thirty centuries.[23] The *nw*-jar phonetic complement and plural strokes found commonly in Dynasties 5 and 6 and New Kingdom writings are not yet attested for this word. Other innovations of the Second Dynasty include the names of foreign countries in association with *inw* and the titles of Egyptian officials connected with this transaction.

The examples of *inw* dating to Dynasty 2 were all discovered on jar labels or sealings. The provenances of the examples, when known, are the royal tomb of Peribsen at Abydos and the Step Pyramid at Saqqara.

11. *Stẖ Pr-ib.sn ḫtmw in(w) Mḥw*
    Seth Peribsen: Seal bearer of the *inw* of Lower Egypt.
    Dyn. 2, Peribsen
    Context: Tomb of Peribsen, Abydos.

12. *. . . inw mḥw . . .*
    . . . *inw* of Lower Egypt . . .
    Dyn. 2, Peribsen[24]
    Context: Tomb of Peribsen, Abydos.

13. *Stẖ Pr-ib.sn inw Sṯt*
    Seth Peribsen: *inw* of Asia.
    Dyn.2, Peribsen[25]

Context: Tomb of Peribsen, Abydos.

14. *nsw-bity [nbty] Sḫm-ib Pr[-n-m3ˁt] in(w) [ḫ3swt] is ḏf3(w)*
King of Upper and Lower Egypt, [The Two Ladies] Sekhem-ib: Per[-en-maat]: *inw* of [foreign lands], storehouse of provisions.
Dyn. 2, Peribsen[26]
Context: Step Pyramid Complex, Saqqara.

15. *Stḫ Pr-ib.sn in(w) Sṯt sš smwt*
Seth Peribsen: *inw* of Asia: scribe of foreign lands.
Dyn. 2, Peribsen[27]
Context: Unknown.

Because the writing of the Second Dynasty more closely followed the conventions of the later periods, the transcriptions here are much surer than those given for Dynasty 1. The sedge-plant was clearly used for *nsw* as can be seen by its pairing with the bee in the expression *nsw-bity*.[28] Further clarity is achieved through writing the names of geographical expressions after the word *inw* rather than before it, as in Dynasty 1. This practice confirms that the transcription *mḥw* for the clump of papyrus is correct.

Clearer organization of the signs in Dynasty 2 also makes it possible to discern formulas used in the transference of *inw*. At least four different formulas were used. They include:

1. King's Name: Official's Title
2. King's Name: Geographical Expression
3. King's Name: Personal Name: Geographical Expression
4. King's Name: Geographical Expression: Official's Title

The formulas were composed of either two or three parts. They all began with the name of the king, showing once again that the king was always either the recipient or donor of *inw*. In the bipartite formulas, the king's name could be followed by an official's title or a geographical expression. In the tripartite formulas, the king's name could be followed by either a personal name plus geographical expression, or a geographical expression plus an official's title.

Though the sample is much too small to draw definitive conclusions, it is interesting that examples of the bipartite formula were found in the tomb of Peribsen at Abydos, whereas the tripartite-formula examples were found in those texts discovered in the Third Dynasty Step Pyramid Complex at Saqqara.

Jars bearing the text of the two-part formulas were obviously intended for royal use. They are all found in an archaeological context that shows their ultimate destination to be the tomb of the king.

The texts bearing the three-part formulas were clearly not discovered in the context for which their writers prepared them. They were all found in the Step Pyramid of Djoser, which had not yet been imagined during the reign of Peribsen. The commodities these jars once held possibly represent royal heirlooms preserved through three or four generations. Another possibility, admittedly very speculative, is that these objects were once redistributed in Dynasty 2 to owners of mastabahs in Saqqara that are no longer preserved. These tombs could have been located on the portion of the Saqqara plateau now occupied by the Step Pyramid Complex.[29] The objects, in this reconstruction of events, would have been reburied by the Dynasty 3 builders of the Step Pyramid. If this hypothesis were correct, it would be evidence for redistribution of *inw* by the king to the officials named in the inscriptions. It would also indicate that different formulas were used for jars intended for royal use and jars intended for redistribution in this period. A third possible explanation for the presence of materials with the name of Peribsen in the Step Pyramid is that they could be related to a cult of this king known to have been active as late as Dynasty 4.[30]

If the titles attested in texts mentioning *inw* in Dynasty 2 do not represent the recipients of the King's redistribution of goods, they probably point to the administrative structure entrusted with seeing to the collection of commodities under this rubric or to the donors. If they are evidence for the administration of *inw,* little more can be said than the "seal bearer of the *inw* of Lower Egypt" and the "scribe of the foreign countries" were involved in the process.[31]

Conversely, the geographical area and individuals named either by title or personal name could represent the donors of *inw* to the king. In this case it would be clear that *inw* could be donated either by foreign countries, provinces of Egypt, or individuals. The implications of this possibility are important for the model of *inw* exchanges originally hypothesized from New Kingdom materials. In the New Kingdom *inw* seems only to have been exchanged between individuals. Foreign donations of *inw* seem to come from the chief of an area rather than from the geographical area itself. Clearly, this observation does not apply in the earliest period.[32]

Dynasty 3

Examples from Dynasty 3 are grouped together with those of Dynasties 1 and 2 because they are more similar in form to the earlier examples than they are to the bulk of Old Kingdom examples. Like the earlier material, the majority of examples of *inw* from Dynasty 3 take the form of jar labels and sealings. The examples can be grouped according to formula types including:

1. *inw* plus personal name
2. *inw* plus estate of an individual
3. *inw* plus institution
4. *inw* plus title and personal name

Inw *Plus Personal Name*

16. *inw Ḫnm-sp.f-ḥr-s3ḥ*
    Inw of Khnum-sepef-her-sakh.
    Dyn. 3, Djoser[33]
    Context: Step Pyramid, Saqqara.

17. *inw Hn<u>t</u>w*
Inw of Hentjew.
Dyn. 3, Djoser[34]
Context: Step Pyramid, Saqqara.

18. *inw Sn-m <u>d</u>.f (?)*
Inw of Sen-medjef (?).
Dyn. 3, Djoser[35]
Context: Step Pyramid, Saqqara.

19. *inw Pt<u>h</u>t<u>h</u>*
Inw of Petkhtekh.
Dyn. 3, Djoser[36]
Context: Step Pyramid, Saqqara.

20. *inw K3k3*
Inw of Kaka.
Dyn. 3, Djoser[37]
Context: Step Pyramid, Saqqara.

21. *inw mitr Sni*
Inw of the palace worker (?) Seni.
Dyn. 3, Djoser[38]
Context: Step Pyramid, Saqqara.

22. *inw Mn<u>t</u>w*
Inw of Mentjew.
Dyn. 3, Djoser[39]
Context: Step Pyramid, Saqqara.

Inw *Plus Estate of an Individual*

23. *inw pr Smn*
Inw of the estate of Semen.
Dyn. 3, Djoser[40]

Context: Step Pyramid, Saqqara.

24. *inw pr ʿḥ3*
Inw of the estate of Aha.
Dyn. 3, Djoser[41]
Context: Step Pyramid, Saqqara.

25. *inw pr Ḥʿ3t*
Inw of the estate of Haat.
Dyn. 3, Djoser[42]
Context: Step Pyramid, Saqqara.

26. *inw pr ʿḥ3-k3*
Inw of the estate of Aha-Ka.
Dyn. 3, Djoser[43]
Context: Step Pyramid, Saqqara.

27. *inw pr Ḥm-nfrt*
Inw of the estate of Hem-neferet.
Dyn. 3, Djoser[44]
Context: Step Pyramid, Saqqara.

28. *inw pr ʿš3-di*
Inw of the estate of Asha-di.
Dyn. 3, Djoser[45]
Context: Step Pyramid, Saqqara.

29. *inw ḥwt (?) wʿb Ḥm*
Inw of the mansion (?) of the priest Hem.
Dyn. 3, Djoser[46]
Context: Step Pyramid, Saqqara.

30. *inẇ pr rsw Sṯt-ḥtp*
Inw of the southern estate of Setjet-hetep.
Dyn. 3, Djoser[47]
Context: Step Pyramid, Saqqara.

Inw *Plus Institution*

31. *inw pr is- ḏf3*
    Inw of the estate of the storehouse of provisions.
    Dyn. 3, Djoser[48]
    Context: Step Pyramid, Saqqara.

32. *inw is ḏf3*
    Inw of the storehouse of provisions.
    Dyn. 3, Djoser[49]
    Context: Step Pyramid, Saqqara.

Inw *Plus Title and Personal Name*

33. *inw ḫr nsw sk-hrw sd sm3 Iy-n-H̱nm*
    Inw belonging to the King; Day of the Sed Festival: the stolistes, Iy-en-Khnum.
    Dyn. 3, Djoser[50]
    Context: Step Pyramid, Saqqara.

34. *inw pr-nsw ḥwt wrt Tti s3b ṯ3yty s3bṯ3y Mn-k3*
    Inw of the estate of the King of the great mansion: He of the Curtain, the Dignitary, the Vizier, Menka.
    Dyn. 3, Djoser[51]
    Context: Step Pyramid, Saqqara.

The division into types of formulas of examples of *inw* belonging to Dynasty 3 yields four types that cannot readily be correlated with the four types of formulas found in Dynasty 2 examples. The material from Dynasty 3 all omitted the king's name, unlike examples of *inw* from Dynasties 1 and 2. In Dynasty 3, in fact, the importance of the king's role in exchanges of *inw* can be determined only from the archaeological context in the Step Pyramid. Additionally, Dynasty 3 examples first record the importance of the individual as the donor of *inw* to the king. Individuals conveyed *inw* to Djoser, indicated in the labels either by personal name, the name of an estate that they held, or through a title plus personal name. At least in the examples found at the Step Pyramid complex, *inw* was not contributed to the King by Upper or Lower Egypt nor by a foreign country. If the evidence quoted here is representative of Dynasty 3 as a whole, it is safe to say that the rules governing exchanges of *inw* that are clear from New Kingdom evidence have begun to emerge in the time of Djoser, though they do not hold universally.

Another important aspect of *inw* from the Step Pyramid complex is found in example 33, which mentions the Sed Festival. Though the connection between *inw* and this festival cannot be explained from this example alone, it is worth noting that the only jar labels of the New Kingdom which preserve the rubric *inw* are dated to the various Sed Festivals of Amenhotep III.

To summarize to this point, *inw* in the first three dynasties began as an exchange between the king and either a province, a foreign country, or an individual. Though most of the extant evidence shows that the king was the primary recipient of *inw,* it is clear that it could be redistributed by the king to his family, officials, and individual commoners. By the Third Dynasty, *inw* donated by individuals to the king appears to have become important, even though the *inw* was said to come from an individual's estate rather than only through the individuals indicated by their names alone.

The Old Kingdom: Dynasties 5 and 6[52]

In and Dynasties 5 and 6, examples of *inw* are more easily read. They were included in longer continuous texts. The writing of the word could include the *nw*-jar with walking legs, the *nw*-jar phonetic complement, and plural strokes. This "standard" writing of *inw* makes it easier for scholars to distinguish the technical term from other passive participles meaning only "that which was brought." The Old Kingdom examples are part of longer continuous texts than the examples found from

Dynasties 1 through 3. They come primarily from the Abu Sir Papyri, the Palermo Stone, and tomb walls. They further demonstrate that *inw* moved in both directions, to and from the king. They also add to our knowledge of the administration of *inw,* both in the royal administration and in private hands.

Inw *for the King from Foreign Countries and Individual Egyptians*

Records of *inw* delivered to the king are preserved both in royal and private inscriptions and in papyrus records during this period.

35. *iwt m w3t tp-sḏb inw in.n.sn n Wsr-K3.f wʿb swt ḫ3stywt 70*
    Coming from the road of Tep-sedjeb, the *inw* that they had brought to Userkaf, pure of places: seventy foreign women.
    Dyn. 5, Userkaf[53]
    Context: Palermo Stone.

36. *inw n smr Nfr.f-rʿ-ʿnḫ s3 k3 1*
    Inw of the courtier Neferefre-ankh: one young bull.
    Dyn. 5/6[54]
    Context: Abu-Sir Papyri.

37. *in.n.i inw nb nfr innw im*
    It was from there that I brought all the good *inw* that was brought.
    Dyn. 5/6[55]
    Context: Tomb of Hekanefer, Toshka West.

38. *I ʿnḫw ii.ty.sn r ḫ3st tn mrrw h3t r nsw ẖr inw.sn n nb.sn . . .*
    Oh, living ones who will come to this hill country, desiring to go down to the King bearing their *inw* to their Lord . . .
    Dyn. 5[56]

Context: Inscription of Shemai, Wadi Hammamat.

39. *innt m inw.k sin(w) iww m ḫrw.k*
That which is being brought is your *inw*. The courtiers who come are your attendants.
Dyn. 5/6, Unas and Teti[57]
Context: Pyramid Texts.

40. *inn ḫrt ḫ3swt nb n nb.f inn inw n ḥkrt-nsw*
One who brings the property of all foreign countries to his Lord. One who brings the *inw* to the Royal Ornament.
Dyn. 6, Merenre and Pepi II[58]
Context: Epithets in the Tomb Biography of Harkhuf, Aswan.

41. The Majesty of Merenre sent me . . . to Yam . . . *in.n.(.i) inw nb(w) im.s nfr ḳꜥḥ ḥs.t(w).i ḥr.s ꜥ3 wrt*
I brought all rare *inw* from it that I might be praised for it greatly.
Dyn. 6, Merenre[59]
Context: Tomb Biography of Harkhuf, Aswan.

42. His Majesty sent me a second time alone . . . *in.n.(i) inw m ḫ3st tn r ꜥ3wt wrt iwty sp int mitt r t3 pn ḏr*
I brought *inw* from this foreign country in great quantity. Never before was the like brought to this entire land.
Dyn. 6, Merenre[60]
Context: Tomb Biography of Harkhuf, Aswan.

43. *ḏd.n.k [r] mḏ3t.k tn wnt in.n.k inw nb ꜥ3 nfr rdi.n Ḥwt- Ḥr nbt Im33w*
You said in this your letter that you brought all the good and great *inw* that Hathor, Mistress of Yamaa, had given.
Dyn. 6, Neferkare-Pepi II[61]
Context: Letter of Neferkare-Pepi II to Harkhuf, Tomb of Harkhuf, Aswan.

44. *[ḫd].k(wi) r.i r inb ḫr inw n ḫ3swt Pnt in ḥ3ty-ᶜ pn w3ḥ.k(wi) inw nb w3ḥ. n it*

I (fa)red [North] to Memphis bearing the *inw* of the foreign countries that this prince brought. I set down all the *inw* which my father set down . . .

Dyn. 6[62]

Context: Tomb Biography of Sabni, Aswan.

45. *km n inw 288*

Total of the *inw*: 228.

Dyn. 5/6[63]

Context: Abu Sir Papyri, list of food accounts.

46. *inw m pr wḏ3w*

Inw from the house of surplus.

Dyn. 5/6[64]

Context: Abu Sir Papyri, a list of officials bringing objects to the storehouse.

47. *[i]nw ḏbt f3it r šnᶜw*

[I]nw: brick that was carried to the storehouse.

Dyn. 5/6[65]

Context: Abu Sir Papyri, rubric over a list of officials' names.

The first example quoted here, from the Palermo Stone, places *inw* in a context familiar from the New Kingdom. This *inw* was brought back from a war with a foreign country. It is here that the historian might first be tempted to translate *inw* as "tribute." Clearly, this translation cannot be appropriate.[66] If *inw* meant tribute, it could not be used to describe both goods that are presented to the king and goods given by the king to others. Because it is clear that the Egyptians called goods moving in either direction *inw,* they must have defined the word without connotations of war, violence, or force. If the concept of tribute existed in ancient Egyptian thought, it must have been expressed by another word.

Moreover, examples from the tomb biographies refer to nonviolently acquired *inw* from both individual Egyptians and foreigners living to the south of Egypt. The only accurate English equivalent to *inw* would be a word that would fit all of the situations in which the Egyptians employed *inw* as an appropriate description of the transaction. From these examples, it is clear the Egyptians saw *inw* as a transaction in which goods moved into or from the king's privy-purse, no matter what the method of acquiring the goods was and without real interest in whether the king ruled over the donor of the goods. This approach allows us to define *inw* from an Egyptian point of view, rather than impose a preconceived idea from a non-Egyptian culture on the sources.

Examples drawn from the Abu Sir Papyri give some insight into the accounts kept of *inw* in the Old Kingdom funerary complex of Neferirkare-kakai. Their context, lists of objects entering and leaving the possession of the royal funerary complex, once again demonstrates that the king is always involved in an exchange of *inw*. These examples also reveal the care with which the Egyptians separated goods that were called *inw* from other commodities.

Individuals are also important as donors of *inw* in the Abu Sir Papyri. Pauline Posener-Kriéger has commented that "the principal interest of this fragment [our example 36] is to show that individuals could make important gifts to the funerary temple of Neferirkare."[67] Additional evidence for the role of individuals is also found in examples 46 and 47. Both of these rubrics are written over the names of officials bringing objects to the storehouse of the royal funerary complex.

Inw *Redistributed in Dynasties 5 and 6*

Inw continues to be found in contexts that demonstrate redistribution to family members of the king, high officials, and workers in the high Old Kingdom.

48. *inw ᶜ mḏ3t 2*
    Inw: two rolls of leather.

Dyn. 5/6[68]

Context: Abu Sir Papyri, from a list of items given to a washerman.

49. *m33 inw n ḥk3.w mniw.f sḫty wḥᶜw innt m ḥwt [. . .]*

Viewing the *inw* of the administrators, shepherds, fowlers, and fishermen, and that which is brought from the estates [. . .]

Dyn. 5, Userkaf[69]

Context: East wall of Tomb of Sekhemkare showing deceased and his wife seated, receiving offering bearers.

50. *m33 nḏt-ḥr inw n ḥwwt T3 Mḥw šmᶜw pr ḏt [i]n ḫry tp nsw . . . Ptḥ-ḥtp . . . m33 iw3 inw n ḏḥwtt m ḥwwt ḥwwt-k3 nt t3 mḥw šmᶜw pr n ḏt . . . m33 nḏt-ḥr 3pdw inw n ḥwwt ḥwwt-k3 nt t3 mḥw šmᶜw pr n ḏt*

Viewing the gifts and *inw* of the estates of Lower and Upper Egypt and the estate [b]y the chief of the royal administration . . . Ptahhotep. Viewing the cattle and the *inw* of the Thoth Festival from the estates and the Mortuary Establishments of Lower and Upper Egypt and the funerary estate. . . . Viewing the the gifts of fowl and the *inw* of the estates, the Mortuary Establishments of Lower and Upper Egypt and the funerary estate.

Dyn. 5, Unis[70]

Context: East wall of Tomb of Ptahhotep II, scene showing tomb owner and son standing, receiving offering bearers.

51. *ip inw niwwt nt ḏt in.n t3 mḥw r prt-ḫrw in s3.f šmsw mry.f s3b ᶜḏ-mr ptḥ-ḥtp . . . ip inw niwwt nt ḏt in.n šmᶜw r prt-ḫrw in s3.f šmsw mry.f s3b ᶜḏ-mr ptḥ-ḥtp*

Counting the *inw* of the funerary domains, which Lower Egypt brought to be invocation offerings, by his eldest son whom he loves, the governor of the province, Ptah-hotep. . . . Counting the *inw* of the funerary domains, which Upper Egypt brought to be invocation offerings, by his eldest son whom he loves, the governor of the province, Ptahhotep.

Dyn. 5, Izezi/Unis[71]

Context: East wall of Tomb of Akhethotep showing deceased receiving offerings and Ptahhotep, son of the deceased, recording offerings.

The example of redistribution in the Abu Sir Papyri of leather rolls to a washerman demonstrates the continued use of *inw* for redistribution from a royal institution to a member of the working class. Though this notation provides little other information, it is comparable to the discovery of *inw* in Saqqara Tomb 230 during the reign of De(we)n, a case of redistribution to a "middle-class" individual.

Dynasty 5, however, does provide a good deal more information about royal redistribution of *inw* to royal family members and high officials. This information is found in scenes of *m33 inw* and *ip inw.*

Royal support of noblemen's funerary establishments has long been recognized. Helene Jacquet-Gordon has observed that a distinctive characteristic of the personified estates depicted in noblemen's tombs during Dynasties 5 and 6 is that "the nobles of the period were benefitting from the generosity of their kings."[72] This generosity is reflected in scenes labeled *m33 inw* in the tombs of Sekhemkare and Ptahhotep II.

The expression *m33 inw,* "seeing," "observing," or "viewing" the *inw* is found twice in Dynasty 5 in scenes belonging to Sekhemkare, the vizier of Userkaf, and Ptahhotep II, the vizier of Izezi or Unis. Both men placed the similarly labeled scenes on the east wall of their funerary chapel. Yvonne Harpur has observed that in general the east wall of an Old Kingdom Memphite tomb is devoted to the presentation of cattle and birds and of the offerings of the personified estates. Workshop and outdoor activities in the marshes are also found in this location.[73] This is true whether or not the scene includes the presentation of *inw.* The east and north walls, as Harpur has discovered, are used to show food acquisition, in contrast to the west and south walls, which depict food presentation to the deceased.[74] This distinction in wall use continues in Memphite tombs even as tombs develop from simple L-shaped chapels into more complex, multiroomed structures.[75]

Harpur's deductions concerning the general use of the east wall in Memphite Old Kingdom tomb chapels place scenes labeled *m33 inw* into the context of food acquisition. These scenes depict the way in which *inw* was acquired by these two men for the support of their tombs, through redistribution from royal institutions. Because royal estates played such a prominent role as the donors of *inw* in these scenes, it becomes clear that in the Old Kingdom, the expression *m33 inw* refers to a tomb owner observing the arrival of royal contributions for the support of his mortuary establishment. The use made of the scene by Old Kingdom tomb owners should not be confused with the execution of the duties of the vizier or *inw* presentation parades found in New Kingdom tombs (see chapter 4).

The origin of Sekhemkare's *inw* offerings is quite clear. Twenty-one male offering bearers are shown arriving from at least seventeen different locations. Fourteen of the names of these locations are compounded with the name of Khafre, the father of Sekhemkare. The objects delivered are all edible tomb offerings. They include fowl—cranes, geese, ducks—and mammals—calves, a gazelle, a hyena, an antelope, and an ibex. Various kinds of fish and baskets of bread complete the register.[76] In this tomb the catch of the clapnet is also included in a separate register in the scene labeled *m33 inw.* Less clearly preserved fishermen are found in a third register. The main caption identifies these products as *inw* as well as those products that clearly derive from royal estates. Perhaps the activities of the fowlers and fishermen are meant to be understood as taking place on the royal estates that are mentioned in the upper register. In any case, such combinations will clearly influence provincial tomb decoration of the First Intermediate Period and Middle Kingdom (see chapter 3).

In the scene of *m33 inw* preserved in the tomb of Ptahhotep II, objects depicted as *inw* are combined with other goods meant to be understood as *nḏt-ḥr* gifts.[77] Of the seven registers depicted as part of Ptahhotep's *m33 inw* scene, the six lower registers include animals reminiscent of those found in Sekhemkare's similarly labeled scene. The uppermost register depicting boys wrestling and the presentation of a boy with his arms bound behind his back requires a broader explanation of the scene.

The six lower registers are an expansion of similar themes in the tomb of Sekhemkare, which dates to early in Dynasty 5. This phenomenon was a common development in tombs of later Dynasty 5.[78] Registers 5 and 7 represent the acquisition of *inw.* The inscriptions included in these two registers refer directly to this fact. Offerings in registers 2, 3, 4, and 6 were by the process of elimination those referred to as *nḏt-ḥr* gifts in the main inscription found over the deceased. There are actually two royal sources for the *inw* delivered to Ptahhotep II. In register 7 the *inw* came from a wide variety of estates and was presented by the Overseer of the Granary of the Mortuary Service, Kehep. This register is comparable to the *inw* shown received by Sekhemkare.

Register 5 however, reveals an additional source of royal *inw* for the deceased. Here a royal official, the King's Companion and Steward Horbity, presented redistributed *inw* from the Thoth Festival. The Thoth Festival was celebrated at the Memphite Royal Residence. The celebration included the transfer of offerings from the Residence to private mortuary establishments.[79] Here clearly was a second way in which the king could redistribute offerings to the deceased under the rubric *inw.*

Registers 2, 3, 4, and 6 reveal other offerings on which the tomb owner depended. Register 2 depicts members of phyles bringing exotic animals. Higher-ranking officials, some of whom were in royal service, presented prestige items such as oryx, ibex, addax, bubalis, and antelope. In this group should be included the Controller of Retainers, Overseer of the Crews, and Chief of the Guard, Neferkhuptah; the Inspector of Retainers, Merer; the Inspector of Retainers, Khay; and the Inspector of Retainers, Mereri. Register 4 is not well preserved.

Register 1 in the *m33 inw* scene of Ptahhotep II is perhaps the most difficult to explain. It depicts twelve nude youths wrestling and six youths accompanying a seventh who is bound. The inscription has been seen by most commentators as mocking the bound youth.[80] Roth has demonstrated at least circumstantially that this scene represents an initiation into a phyle. Thus the whole wall shows the establishment of the phyle and the sources of the offerings which the phyle members will present to the deceased. *Inw* is one of those sources.

Although the tomb scenes of Sekhemkare and Ptahhotep II are related by their common caption, the double scene of counting the *inw* found in the tomb of Akhethotep also adds to the evidence that *inw* was donated by the king to the deceased in some cases. Here personified royal estates bring commodities to the son of the tomb owner who records them. This scene forms the lowest register of a larger, east-wall food-acquisition scene. Each half of the scene depicts thirteen personified estates. The left half of the scene at least partially preserves labels for all of the figures. Eleven of the names of the estates are compounded with royal names. In the right half of the scene, only five labels are preserved. Here three place names are compounded with a royal name. The wide variety of offerings preserved in this scene is again a clear association between royal gifts to the deceased and the rubric *inw.*

Conclusions about *Inw* in the First Six Dynasties

A review of the model for ancient Egyptian economic transactions is in order before evaluating its accuracy for each of the periods under discussion here. The first hypothesis proposed was that ancient Egyptian economic exchanges were named according to the sociopolitical position of the donor and recipient. They were governed by social relationships rather than economic relationships as understood in the modern world. Second, economic exchanges were named according to the use of the commodities exchanged. Exchanges of commodities circulated through the royal privy-purse were given a different name from other exchanges.

The first hypothesis as it concerns *inw* was that the sociopolitical positions involved in these exchanges were the king and almost anyone else. In the First Dynasty, donors were not specifically mentioned in the labels, though the royal connection was well established. Even in examples found in nonroyal archaeological contexts, no individual, Egyptian province, or foreign country was specifically named. Only the name of the king and the fact that the *inw* either went to or came from him was clearly articulated. In Dynasty 2, the king's name was always stressed, but expanded information concerning the donor was included in the labels. Officials' titles, geographical expressions both domestic and foreign, personal names, and various combinations of these three bits of data were found following the king's name. It is likely that the order in which this additional information was written, if understood, would reveal the direction in which the goods flowed and the administrator responsible for the transaction. The bipartite formulas were all found in an archaeological context, suggesting royal use of the *inw*. The tripartite formulas were all found in a context that might suggest that they were redistributed. This idea, however, remains highly speculative. The meaning of writing the personal name before the geographical expression (type 3) and vice versa (type 4) has not been established. With the present limited data, it seems unlikely that this question can be resolved.

By Dynasty 3, individual Egyptians donated *inw* to the king. They donated both personally and through their estates. The king's name, however, is omitted from Third Dynasty jar labels and sealings. The only way to establish royal use for these commodities is the archaeological context. The first hint that the *sed*-festival was one important occasion for individuals to donate *inw* to the king is also found in this collection of texts.

Evidence from the Old Kingdom came from a wide range of contexts. The accounts of the Abu Sir Papyri, the royal records of the Palermo Stone, and tombs of noblemen both in captions and extended texts present a fuller picture of the donors and recipients of *inw*. *Inw* could be acquired through war with foreigners, nonviolent expeditions to foreign countries, and Egyptian individuals. This wide range of donors, all subordinate to the king in Egyptian ideology, were considered to be equals in their subservience. It is most likely that the sociopolitical status of the donors of commodities to the king accounted for the Egyptian use of the word *inw* to describe the transactions which occurred.

Redistribution of the king's *inw*, its restricted use according to the second hypothesis, was also evident in the periods under discussion. This was established through archaeological context in the earlier periods (Dynasties 1 through 3) and explicit statements in the accounting texts of Abu Sir for the Old Kingdom. *Inw* was found in the tombs of royal family members, high officials, and commoners. The method of redistribution in the earlier period is completely unknown. It may have been relatively rare. During the Old Kingdom, the evidence for redistribution to high officials highlights the role of royal mortuary establishments. The royal funeral domains were the source for royal *inw* delivered to Sekhemkare, Akhethotep, and Ptahhotep II; they were depicted as personified estates.

Though little is known of the officials who administered *inw* in this period, the administrative distinction between *inw* commodities and commodities exchanged under other rubrics was well established by Dynasty 5. Within the royal bureaucracy, *inw* was separately noted from *ᶜḳw, 3wt,* and from *ḥtp-nṯr.*[81] Within private circles, *inw* was kept separate from *prt-ḫrw* and *nḏt-ḥr* offerings. Both of these other offerings were received from the estates and towns specifically assigned to the support of a nobleman's tomb.[82] This administrative separation of *inw* and other types of commodity exchanges assures modern readers that it meant something very specific to the Egyptians: an exchange between the king and others that could be redistributed.

Chapter Three

Inw *during the First Intermediate Period and the Middle Kingdom: A Broadening Concept*

The collapse of the central government at the end of Dynasty 6 resulted in a concurrent eclipse of the system governing the collection and redistribution of *inw*. Though *The Instructions for Merikare* reported delivery of *inw* during Dynasty 9/10, it remains likely that this royal prerogative was limited in scope, as were other aspects of kingship during the First Intermediate Period. Tefibi of Siut, though he is only a nomarch, certainly believed that he was entitled to this same privilege.

The reestablishment of kingship by the princes of Thebes during Dynasty 11 witnessed the reinstatement of *inw* collection and redistribution within their own area of hegemony. Inscriptions from Thebes dating to this period reflect a situation similar to the Old Kingdom regarding *inw* collection. In reality, during the years intervening between Dynasties 6 and 11, *inw* collection and redistribution had become a function of the nomarchs along with other royal attributes.[1] As long as the local lords maintained hegemony in their nomes, they continued to collect *inw* in the manner of royalty. The examples quoted here show a new attitude toward *inw* revealing the early Middle Kingdom tendency of nomarchs to assume royal prerogatives, which in turn led to an expanded view of the meaning of *inw*. This broadening led to a limited, nontechnical use of this term attested in literary texts during the Middle Kingdom.

The following chapter examines both the traditional, normative uses of the word *inw* based on Old Kingdom models and new uses of the word that arose during the First Intermediate Period and continued into the Middle Kingdom. A discussion of redistribution of *inw* at the royal center, including both the palace and the mortuary temple, follows.

The First Intermediate Period

The First Intermediate Period witnessed a breakdown in Egyptian society's expectations of government. Whether or not the period was one of total disorder, the normal functioning of the central government ceased. The contrast between Old Kingdom and First Intermediate Period economic arrangements could not be more clear than in the following examples.

1. *nfrw n.k ḥnʿ ʿ-rsy iw n.k ẖr g3wt ẖr inw*
   Be good (or it is well with you) together with the Southland, which comes to you bearing dues and bearing *inw*.
   Dyn. 9–10, Instructions for Merikare[2]
   Context: Wisdom text.

2. *n sẖm(.i) r nḏs ḥr-iwtt ḫpr.f r(.i) m sprti in inw.w*
   (I) was not impetuous against a commoner because of the way he did not appear to (me) as a petitioner who brought *inw*.
   Dynasty 9/10[3]
   Context: Tomb biography of Tefibi of Siut.

The assumptions about *inw* that are clear in the *Instructions for Merikare* parallel the Old Kingdom practice of *inw* exchange. Here the Old Kingdom exchange between the king and a person or group of lower social status remained intact. Tefibi of Siut, however, probably expressed a more widespread view of the meaning of *inw* at this time. During roughly the same period, Tefibi believed that a nomarch could also expect *inw* for himself without the involvement of the king. Clearly the definition of *inw* had been widened to include an exchange between persons of unequal social status, whether or not one of the parties to the exchange was the king of a united Egypt. This broadening will later be reflected in the sources from Dynasty 11 and early Dynasty 12.

The Early Middle Kingdom

Inw *for the King*

Traditional Exchanges of Inw *for the King at Thebes in Dynasty 11*

The normative Old Kingdom meaning of *inw,* goods exchanged between the king and his sociopolitical inferiors, was certainly revived by the Theban kings of Dynasty 11. The following examples demonstrate that the royal *inw* could be collected from both individuals and geographical areas during the Middle Kingdom.

3. *iw sʿ3.n.f w(i) sḫnt.n.f st.(i) di.n.f w(i) m st ḫrt-ib.f m ʿḥ.f n wʿʿw sḏ3wt m-ʿ.(i) ẖr ḏbʿt.(i) m stpw n nfrt nbt innt n ḥm n nb.i m šmʿw m t3-mḥw m sšr nb n sḫmḫ-ib m inw n t3 pn mi ḳd.f n snḏw.f ḫtḫt t3 pn innt n ḥm n nb.(i) m-ʿ ḥḳ3w ḥryw-tp dšrt n snḏw.f ḫtḫt ḫ3swt*

   He made me great after he had advanced my station and after he had taken me into his confidence in his palace of privacy, while precious things were in my charge under my seal, even the choicest of every good thing that was brought to the Majesty of my lord from Upper Egypt and Lower Egypt consisting of every good thing that gives pleasure, the *inw* of this entire land because of the fear of him throughout this land, and that which was brought to the Majesty of my lord by the hand of the chieftains who rule over the Red Land, and because of the fear of him throughout the foreign countries.

Dyn. 11, Inyotef II-III[4]
Context: Stele of Tjetji.

4. *ḫtmty bity smr-wᶜty imy-r pr ḥnw ḏd iw h3b.[n w(i)] nb.(i) ᶜ.w.s. r sbt kbnwyt r Pwnt r int n.f ᶜntyw w3ḏ m-ᶜ ḥḳ3w ḥry-tp dšrt n snḏ.f ḫt ḫ3swt . . . ḫr ḫt iwt.(i) m w3ḏ-wr ir.n.(i) wḏt n ḥm.f in.n.(i) n.f inw nb gm.n.i ḥr idbw t3-nṯr*

The Royal Seal Bearer, Sole Companion, Overseer of the House, Henou says: My lord, l.p.h., sent me in order to dispatch *kpny*-boats to Punt in order to bring for him fresh myrrh from the rulers who are over the Red Land, his fear being throughout the foreign countries. . . . After I came from the sea (I) performed the command of H.M., I having brought to him all the *inw* (I) found on the shores of God's-land.

Dyn. 11, Mentuhotep III (*Sᶜnḫ-k3-rᶜ*)[5]
Context: Inscription from the Wadi Hammamat of Year 8.

These two texts of Dynasty 11 made claims for the king receiving *inw* that were completely traditional. In the *Tjetji Stele*, *inw* came from both Upper and Lower Egypt as well as the Rulers of the Red Land (Punt?). The nobleman Henou made similar claims for his sovereign Seankhkare Mentuhotep. Yet evidence from Memphis shows that the situation was more complex. The traditional meaning of *inw* had expanded even at the center, perhaps as a result of events in the provinces during Dynasty 11.

Inw *for the King from Nature*

5. *inw Wḥᶜ-Nbty m i3dt 12 n ᶜḳw 3pd.w 11,350 inw n [. . .] in.w 458*

Inw of the Fisher-Fowler of the Two Ladies [i.e., the King] with twelve nets; the birds that entered 11,350. *Inw* of [. . .] fish 458

Dynasty 12, Amenemhet II[6]
Context: Royal annals.

Amenemhet's II annalistic inscription revealed an additional context for *inw* at the royal center. In this document, the king gathered *inw* from nature rather than from other people. The king performed this act as the "Fisher-Fowler of the Two Ladies," a rare epithet known from a contemporary literary text and from a statue of the time of Amenhotep II. The literary text is too fragmentary to translate, but the New Kingdom text makes clear that this is a guise of the king that stressed his physical prowess. The texts called the "Fisher-Fowler of the Two Ladies" the *ir m ᶜ.wy.fy*, "the one who acts with his two arms."

Evidence does not exist to establish whether this sort of act of physical prowess had roots in the Old Kingdom or if this description of the king was an innovation of Dynasty 12. If indeed he was performing a new royal ritual, it was most likely a result of the reshaping of the descriptions of *inw* redistribution by local rulers such as those at Beni Hasan, Meir, and Bersheh during Dynasty 11 and the start of Dynasty 12.

Provincial Exchanges of **Inw** *in Dynasty 11 and Early Dynasty 12: From Redistribution to Local Autonomy for the Nomarch*

There were two kinds of royal redistribution of *inw* depicted in Old Kingdom tombs. They included the scene of the Thoth Festival in Ptahhotep II's tomb and a clapnet scene in Sekhemkare's tomb. Both scenes have been discussed in chapter 1 as aspects of food production for the deceased, typically found on the east wall of a Memphite mastabah. Both Old Kingdom scenes attested to the royal source of goods called *inw*. In the Middle Kingdom, both kinds of scenes are preserved by local rulers. Whether local rulers at Beni Hasan, Meir, and Bersheh thought these scenes depicted gifts from the king or were due to them directly from local temples or nature as independent rulers must have varied by time and place. Each type of scene will be discussed separately.

Inw *Received at a Festival for the Nomarch*

6. *m33 inw k3w iw3w wnḏw*

Inspecting the *inw* of bulls, long horned cattle, and short horned cattle.
Dynasty First Intermediate Period/Early Middle Kingdom[7]
Context: Caption on south wall of tomb of Baqet I (Beni Hasan tomb 29).

7. *inw sẖpt n k3 n Snbi m3ᶜ-ḫrw*
Inw: conducted to the *ku* of Senbi, justified.
Amenemhet I[8]
Context: Caption in the tomb of Senbi, son of Ukhhotep (Meir Tomb Chapel B1).

8. *inw n nb(t) ḥb n k3w.k . . . inw n sẖt n k3.k*
Inw of the Mistress of the festival for your *ku*'s . . . *inw* of the marshland for your *ku.*
Amenemhet I[9]
Context: Caption from the tomb of Senbi, son of Ukhhotep (Meir Tomb Chapel B1).

9. *n k3.k inw nfr ḥ3t sẖt*
For your *ku* the best of the *inw* of the field.
Senwosret I[10]
Context: Caption from the North wall in front of an offering bearer, tomb of Ukhhotep I son of Senbi (Meir Tomb Chapel B2).

10. *inw nfr n sẖt n ḥ3ty-ᶜ Wẖ-ḥtp*
Good *inw* of the field for the local prince Ukhhotep.
Senwosret I[11]
Context: Caption in statue recess, north wall, the tomb of Ukhhotep I son of Senbi (Meir Tomb Chapel B2).

11. *inw n nbt ḥb n k3.k*
Inw of the Mistress of the Festival for your *ku.*
Senwosret I[12]

Context: Caption in the statue niche, west wall tomb of Ukhhotep son of Senbi (Meir Tomb Chapel B2).

Scenes of *inw* delivered to local rulers depicting a festival are related to the same tradition as that found in Ptahhotep II's tomb. It is impossible to argue for direct dependence of the Middle Kingdom examples on a particular Old Kingdom tomb. Yet the artist of each tomb must have found inspiration in a common tradition. That tradition included depictions of *inw* inspection by the deceased along with an upper register of wrestling youths. The Middle Kingdom tombs containing this scene began in late Dynasty 11 (reign of Mentuhotep IV?) and continued into the reigns of Amenemhet I and Senwosret I.[13] The oldest of the Middle Kingdom tombs, belonging to Baqet I, preserved two scenes of inspecting or observing the *inw* by the deceased. One scene included wrestling and one scene depicted *inw* from the clapnet. These two scenes demonstrate both the hold of tradition on the local ruler in Beni Hasan and the inevitable changes occurring through time as old concepts developed and broadened with extended use.

On the south wall at its western end, Baqet I stands before four registers. The accompanying caption gives his titles. Smaller inscriptions in each register, oriented toward the figure of Baqet, record that he is inspecting the *inw*. The general arrangement of the registers in this scene parallels the similarly labeled scene of inspecting *inw* in the tomb of Ptahhotep II at Saqqara. Though Ptahhotep's tomb is more elaborately decorated and contains seven registers in contrast to Baqet I's four, the general arrangement is similar. There are wrestlers in the uppermost register and a similar ordering of animals depicting gazelles followed by cattle. The scene is very traditional; a provincial ruler of late Dynasty 11 has chosen the iconography common to the tomb of a high official of the Old Kingdom. One important difference separates these scenes, however. In the tomb of Ptahhotep II, the source of the *inw* is the royal estates. Baqet I's *inw* has no clear donor other than nature itself.

The north walls of Senbi and Ukhhotep I's tombs—two generations of rulers at Meir—also share iconographical similarities with the scene in Ptahhotep II's and Baqet I's tombs. Again, no direct stylistic dependence is discernible in the relationship between the tombs of Baqet I and the two rulers in Meir, even though they are closer in time to each other than either is to the tomb of Ptahhotep II. Yet there is a clear dependence in the Meir tombs on the same tradition, which placed inspecting or viewing *inw* in a context that included wrestling.

In chapter 2, wrestling and the subsequent mocking of the defeated was considered a possible representation of initiation into the phyle. The other major event mentioned in Ptahhotep II's *inw* scene is the Thoth Festival. The scene of initiation and deliveries from the Thoth Festival could thus be considered two components of one festival. This conjecture is strengthened by the presence of wrestling scenes at other festivals. The tomb of Senbi, for example, depicts wrestling as part of the local Hathor Festival where the deceased also views *inw.*[14] In the New Kingdom, wrestling is associated the New Year Festival and other royal appearances.[15] Thus *inw* presentation/inspection/viewing scenes that included a register of wrestlers might well be considered depictions of festivals.

The Hathor Festival at Meir was a local occasion for collecting *inw.* The absence of royal donations in these scenes argues that Baqet I, Senbi, and Ukhhotep I regarded the presentation of *inw* to them directly from nature as their right as local potentates. Yet it is striking that the basic iconography employed here was so similar to the scene of royal redistribution of *inw* in Ptahhotep's tomb depicting the Thoth Festival. An older tradition was here transformed for contemporary circumstances. A scene of redistribution from royal sources has become an assertion of local autonomy and control over nature.

Inw *from Nature: A Royal or Provincial Custom?* *Inw* from nature consists most often of birds or fish captured with the clapnet. This type of scene occasionally included some desert animals from the hunt. It is found in the following Middle Kingdom examples.

12. *m33 inw ꜥwt ḫ3st s3w sšw sḫwt . . . [in] ḥ3ty-ꜥ rḫ-nsw mr.f ḥs B[3]ḳt*

    Inspecting the *inw* of the wild animals, the pools, the marshes, and the snare . . . [by] the local Prince, One Known to the King, one whom he loves, one who is praised, Baqet.

    Dynasty 11[16]

    Context: Caption on the north wall in tomb of Baqet I (Beni Hasan Tomb 29).

13. *m3(3) inw.w ꜥwt ḫ3st in ḥ3m š3w sšw sḫwt n spḥw mrw (i)n ḥ3ty-ꜥ ḫtmty smr-wꜥt ḥry-tp ꜥ3 m M3-ḥḏ B3ḳt*

    Inspecting the *inw* of wild game by fish catching, the pool, the marshes, the snares of the lassoes, and the canals, by the local Prince, Royal Seal Bearer, Sole Companion, and Great Chief of the Oryx nome, Baqet.

    Dynasty 11[17]

    Context: Caption on the north wall of tomb of Baqet II (Beni Hasan Tomb 33).

Inw redistributed from the hunt, fowling, or fishing perhaps derives from a tradition reflected in the tomb of Sekhemkare at Giza (see chapter 2). This royal descendant of Menkare, who served as a high official during early Dynasty 5, was depicted inspecting or viewing *inw* from royal estates delivered to his offering table. Sekhemkare's *inw* included birds from the clapnet, though in the scene it was made clear that these gifts came to the deceased through royal redistribution.

Baqet I and Baqet II of Beni Hasan each included a scene of inspecting *inw* from the hunt in their tombs, but without any indication of the identity of the donor aside from nature.[18] These two tombs, which clearly do have a direct dependence, depicted the standing figure of the deceased receiving the animals caught in the desert hunt, birds from the clapnet, and fish from the fishing net.

Scenes of observing fishing and fowling in the marshes were common from Old Kingdom tombs. But these early scenes were rarely labeled under the rubric *inw*. In fact, Sekhemkare's *inw* inspection is anomalous, because he sat at the offering table while he inspected. This posture is perhaps unique to scenes captioned *m33*. A much commoner Old Kingdom tradition is found in the tomb of Niankhkhnum. Here a scene depicting a nobleman overseeing bird trapping and fishing is described in the caption as, "Seeing the fields, the marshlands, the catch of fish, the trapping of fowl. See, it is more beautiful than anything."[19] The term *inw* was not used in such scenes to describe products that the deceased received or viewed during the Old Kingdom unless the donor was royal.

Thus the Middle Kingdom depiction of hunting, bird trapping, and fishing was a distinct broadening of the meaning of *inw*. It is easy to understand that this use of the word might be the beginning of a broader use of the term to mean "products" or the "yield" of the desert, marsh, or river in literary contexts. Yet there is some evidence that these local rulers understood the use of the term *inw* in this context to be a prerogative of the ruler. Hartwig Altenmüller and Ahmed Moussa make clear that Amenemhet II described in his annals a ceremony of bird trapping and fishing. In this ceremony, the king described the catch as *inw*. After the ceremony the followers of the king were formally rewarded.[20] It seems likely that Amenemhet II based his own ceremony on a provincial custom, unknown to the Old Kingdom, that asserted the ruler's position over nature by associating the catch with the ancient *inw* gift from a human to the king.

The tomb of Baqet I, by preserving a scene both of the festival setting for transmission of *inw* and a nature ceremony of trapping and fishing, preserves a complete early Middle Kingdom view of *inw* at the end of Dynasty 11. This view then continued into Dynasty 12. The next generation, however, took a more conservative view of *inw* transmission, converting this scene into a means of expressing loyalty to the king.

Dynasty 12

Traditional Inw *for the King from Provincial Sources*

As the kings of Dynasty 12 strengthened their control over the country, local rulers made statements clearly supporting the traditional vision of *inw* exchanges between individual people or places and the king. Provincial rulers, however, continued to claim the right to nature's *inw* for themselves, but now probably viewed this ceremony as an outgrowth of a royal policy.

14. *šms.(kw)i nb.i ḫft ḫnt.f r sḥrt ḫftyw.f m ḫ3swt . . . sn.[i] k3š m ḫntyt in.n.i ḏrw t3 in.n.i inw nb.i*

    I followed my lord when he sailed upstream to overthrow his enemies in the foreign countries. . . . I passed through Kush while sailing upstream. No sooner did I conquer the boundary of the land than I acquired the *inw* of my lord.

    Dyn. 12, Senwosret I[21]

    Context: Tomb No. 2 at Beni Hasan, the nomarch Amenemhet.

15. *ḥr ḏbʿwt(.f) m ḫrt nb(t) [ḫ3swt] m ipt-nsw smi [.n].f inw Mḏ3 m b3kwt ḥk3w ḫ3swt*

    ". . . under his seal in every *ḫrt*-impost of the foreign countries in the royal counting-house. One to whom is reported the *inw* of the Medjai and the *b3kwt* of the Rulers of foreign countries."

    Senwosret I[22]

    Context: Tomb Biography of Sirenput I of Aswan.

16. *[. . .]t ḥnʿ inw.sn ḫrt hrw nt rʿ nb ip[.f st] n nsw n ḏtḏt*

    . . . together with their *inw* of every day which he assesses for the king forever.

Dyn. 12, Amenemhet II–Senwosret II–III[23]
Context: Biography of the nomarch Djheutyhotep II of Bersheh, over individuals labeled with titles.

During early Dynasty 12, the central government was able to extend its influence to the point that normative statements about *inw* were made once again in some nomes. Amenemhet of Beni Hasan, Sirenput II of Aswan, and Djeheutyhotep II of Bersheh all speak about *inw* in a way that shows that its exchange was an essential element in each man's relationship with the king.

There are relatively few monumental inscriptions from this period describing the delivery of *inw* to the king at the capital. Due to the accidents of preservation, discovery, and publication, more monumental inscriptions from Old Kingdom tombs and New Kingdom historical inscriptions can be quoted to describe the act of delivering *inw* to the king. The examples quoted here, however, conform to the general pattern found in the Old Kingdom and revived in the Theban area during Dynasty 11. The *inw* was delivered to the king and was considered to be his property. Within Egypt, the donors were described as geographical expressions such as the Southland (*ᶜ-rsy*) or Upper and Lower Egypt (*šmᶜw* and *t3-mḥw*). Foreign *inw* arrived from Kush. In spite of this mode of description of the delivery of *inw* to the king, example 14 possibly explains the ultimate origin of *inw* within Egypt. Here in the tomb of Amenemhet of Beni Hasan, the tomb owner is shown assessing *inw* of specific individuals. Yet the inscription makes clear that this *inw* was for the king. Examples that refer to deliveries from Upper and Lower Egypt or from administrative departments must then refer to assessments made on individuals, which are delivered to the king by the nomarch as their representative. The individual's names might even have been recorded as they gave the *inw* and this information could have found its way into royal account texts. The same concept of individuals bringing *inw* to the nomarch was found at Bersheh in the tomb of Djeheutyhotep II. Here individually named officials convey *inw* to the local government for eventual delivery to the king.

Provincial Inw *Exchanges for the Nomarch in Dynasty 12: From Local Autonomy to Redistribution for Local Rulers*

In spite of these normative examples of *inw* conveyed to the king, nomarchs continue to claim the right to *inw* from nature early in Dynasty 12.

17. *r ṯrp n k3.k inw nb nfr n sḫt n k3.k*
    Goose [*Anser anser*] and goose [*Anser albifrons*] for your *ku.* All good *inw* of the marsh for your *ku.*
    Dynasty 11/Dynasty 12[24]
    Context: Caption, south wall, over man carrying geese to standing figure of Baqet III (Beni Hasan Tomb 15).

18. *sẖpt inw nb nfr r ḥwt-ᶜ3t n k3 n ḥ3ty-ᶜ Imny m3ᶜ-ḫrw*
    Conducting all good *inw* to the tomb chapel for the *ku* of the local Prince, Ameny, justified.
    Senwosret I[25]
    Context: Part of the calendar of offerings on the south wall of the tomb of Amenemhet (Beni Hasan Tomb 2).

19. *sẖpt inw nb nfr r ḥwtin ᶜ3t n k3 n im3ḫt nbt pr Ḥtpt m3ᶜt-ḫrw . . . sẖpt inw nb nfr n ḥbnw n k3.s in ḥk3 ḥwt Iḳry*
    Conducting all good *inw* to the tomb chapel for the *ku* of the honored one, the Mistress of the House Hetepet, justified . . . conducting all good *inw* of Hebnu for her *ku* by the district Governor, Iqrey.
    Senwosret I[26]
    Context: Two captions describing deliveries to the offering table of the Lady Hetepet in the Tomb of Amenemhet (Beni Hasan Tomb 2).

20. *sẖpt inw nb nfr r ḥwt-ᶜ3 n k3 n ḥ3ty-ᶜ Imn-m-ḥ3t*
    Conducting all the good *inw* to the tomb chapel for the *ku* of the nomarch Amenemhet.
    Senwosret I[27]

Context: Caption over the offerings for Amenemhet's offering table in his tomb (Beni Hasan Tomb 2).

21. *m33 inw nb nfr [in].n.f m niwt.f m sp3t.f nt ẖnw M3-ḥḏ in iry-pꜥt ḥ3ty-ꜥ ḫtmty bity smr wꜥt imy-r ḥm-nṯr n ḥr (?)*
Viewing of all the good *inw* he (i.e., Khnumhotep II) had brought from his towns and his nomes of the interior of the Oryx nome by the Hereditary Noble, local Prince, Royal Seal Bearer, Sole Companion, Overseer of Priests of Horus (?), (Khnumhotep).
Senwosret II[28]
Context: Ancestors of Khnumhotep viewing the offering table in the tomb of Netjernakht (Beni Hasan Tomb 23).

22. *ky smsw m nḏw m smr-wꜥty ꜥ3 imy n smrw ꜥš3 inw pr-nsw*
Another elder (son) is a protector and sole companion, great among the companions, rich in the *inw* of the palace.
Reign of Senwosret II[29]
Context: Autobiography of Khnumhotep II of Beni Hasan (Beni Hasan Tomb 3).

23. *m33 irt irw m mnmnwt nb(w)t inw in n.f m niwt.f sp3wt.f nt ẖnw m3-ḥḏ.f in iry-pꜥt ḥ3ty-ꜥ ḥri s3 ẖnm-ḥtp m3ꜥ-ḫrw*
Watching the levying of the cattle tax on all the cattle, and the *inw* which was brought to him from his town and his districts of the interior of his Oryx-nome by the Hereditary Noble, local Prince Heri's son, Khnumhotep, justified.
Senwosret II[30]
Context: Caption from the tomb of Khnumhotep II (Beni Hasan Tomb 3).

24. *n k3.k inw n sḫt*
For your *ku, inw* of the marsh.
Amenemhet II–Senwosret III[31]

Context: Caption in the tomb of Djheutyhotep II (Bersheh Tomb 2).

25. *ḥtpt ḏf3w ꜥwt nbt iw3w ḥ3t mḏwt inw nb nfr imy idḥ n k3 n ḥ3ty-ꜥ imy-r3 ḥmw-nṯr wḫ-ḥtp s3 wḫ-ḥtp*
Offerings, supplies, all small cattle, oxen, the best of the stalled cattle, all the good *inw* which is in the Delta marshes for the *ku* of the local Prince, Overseer of Priests, Ukhhotep's son, Ukhhotep.
Senwosret II[32]
Context: Caption over men and women making offerings to Ukhhotep II (Meir Tomb Chapel C.1).

26. *[3pd]w ꜥ3 wrt [in]w nb nfr n sḫwt imyt T3-mḥw sḏf3w.n wḏḥw sḫb.n wsḫt iry-pꜥt ḥ3ty-ꜥ [. . .] Wḫ-ḥtp ms n Ḥny-ḥr-ib*
Very numerous [fowl], all good [*in*]*w* of the marshlands that are in the Delta, that we might provision the offering table and that we might adorn the broad court (for) the Hereditary Noble, local Prince, [. . .] Ukhhotep, born of Henyherib.
Senwosret II[33]
Context: Caption over women with fowl in baskets from tomb of Ukhhotep II (Meir Tomb Chapel C.1).

The reemergence of the normative Old Kingdom view of *inw* redistribution to local rulers is well documented in provincial tombs. There is a clear sequence of tombs in which this trend can be seen. Starting with Baqet III of Beni Hasan, there is a tendency to combine the festival distribution of *inw* with the clapnet scene in provincial tombs. By the time of Khnumhotep II and his son, Khnumhotep III, who is mentioned in his father's biography, the normative statements about *inw* as a royal prerogative have returned and the royal source of *inw* is acknowledged in the provincial tombs.

The tomb of Baqet III (B.H. Tomb 15) mentions *inw* only once in contrast to the tomb of his ancestor Baqet I (B.H. Tomb 29).

The text is found on the south wall, the area where Baqet I depicted the festival scene that combined wrestling and *inw* presentation. Baqet III depicted the trapping of fowl and net fishing in contrast to Baqet I and Baqet II, who had placed this scene on the north wall. Aside from a possible pun on the word *ḥb* (*Wb.* III, 62), meaning "catch," with *ḥb* (*Wb.* III, 57), meaning "festival," in register four of the subscene, it seems likely that the term *inw* has been buried on this wall away from its usual Middle Kingdom context. There is neither a festival including wrestling nor a hunting/nature festival depicted here. The label for the subscene reads "Observing/Inspecting the work of the marshes by . . . Baqet [III]." This caption signals a gradual return to the ideas about *inw* prevalent during the Old Kingdom. The inscription recalls that of Niankhkhnum's east wall where activities in the field were related to food production only, without reference to redistributive festivals or to the king.

Proceeding chronologically, the next Beni Hasan tomb to mention *inw* belonged to the nomarch Amenemhet (Tomb 2). *Inw* is found in this tomb describing offerings to the deceased and his wife three times. Here there is no sign of any kind of festival of redistribution. There is an emphasis here on *inw* as offerings at the tomb chapel, an emphasis that is more explicit here than it was earlier in the Middle Kingdom. This *inw* is not connected to other humans or to nature directly. Possibly Amenemhet avoided mentioning the source in an attempt neither to claim *inw* as a local ruler nor to acknowledge the royal prerogative.[34] Alternatively, it could be a nontechnical use of the term, which relies on the original etymology for its meaning, "that which is brought."

The tomb of Netjernakht of Beni Hasan (Tomb 23) contains a poorly preserved scene of the deceased inspecting the *inw* intended for his offering table. As was the case in the tomb of Amenemhet, there is no indication of a festival of any sort or of a royal donor. This tomb, like that of Amenemhet, probably represents a stage in the history of *inw* where the technical term had been abandoned for a more neutral participle meaning "products."

Three roughly contemporary tombs, ranging in date from the reigns of Amenemhet II through Senwosret III, demonstrate a return to traditional ideas about *inw* immediately before the disappearance of the provincial rulers' tombs in the Middle Kingdom. Khnumhotep II of Beni Hasan, Djeheutyhotep II of Bersheh, and Ukhhotep II of Meir each took a different approach to decorating their tombs as they adjusted to an increasingly powerful central government. Beginning with Khnumhotep II, provincial tombs depicted both a festival context and royal participation in the delivery of *inw* to the deceased.

The much-discussed north wall of Khnumhotep II's tomb at Beni Hasan reintroduces the depiction of *inw* redistributed at a festival.[35] Dieter Kessler has identified this festival as a local New Year's ritual, though royal participation is a factor.[36] Kessler associates the cattle count mentioned in the main inscription—part of what the deceased "views"—with the New Year's Festival. If this identification is correct, another part of this festival is the hunt in the desert and the clapnet scene. Khnumhotep II watches himself as he hunts wild game with a bow in the company of his four sons. The clapnet scene is also included here, relating this scene to a tradition of viewing *inw* as early as Baqet I in Beni Hasan.

The absence of wrestling figures here might point to a recognition of royal prerogatives. Wolfgang Decker believes that rituals that included wrestling were performed only in the presence of the king. The omission of wrestling here contrasts with what is found in the tombs of the more independent nomarchs Baqet I and Ukhhotep I when they observed *inw*. This is the first indication at Beni Hasan of some deference to royal authority.

The presence of the Royal Scribe Neferhotep in the fourth register, directly before the deceased and leading the famous Asiatic caravan, indicated even more strongly the acknowledgment that the king had an integral role in exchanges of *inw*. Khnumhotep II clarified his understanding of *inw* in his autobiographical inscription. There he discussed the wealth of his son Khnumhotep III, part of which derived from the "*inw* of the palace." The link between *inw* redistribution and royal gifts is fully acknowledged here. Khnumhotep presented himself viewing *inw* and participating in the hunt, probably a reference to the same sort of festival which Amenemhet II celebrated at Memphis. It is possible, though not demonstrable, that Khnumhotep II considered himself to be part of a royal ceremony in this scene.

Djeheutyhotep II of Bersheh was a contemporary of Khnumhotep II of Beni Hasan. The north wall of his tomb also depicts a similar link between *inw* and a festival of fishing and fowling. On the north wall of his inner chamber, Djeheutyhotep stands observing himself and his sons trap fowl with the clapnet. The fowl is then presented to his *ku* as *inw* of the marsh.

Beneath the clapnet is an inscription that might refer to the name of this festival. It reads,

> *mk di n.n Sḫt ʿ sn[fr] ḥb[s]ḫt n.s iit m ḥtp n smr pn wrw 5 m [pr] ḏḥwty ḥs.s mr.s ḥ3ty-ʿ ḏḥwty-ḥtp*, "Look, Sekhet [the personified marsh] gives a hand to us. Carry out the Festival/Catch of Sekhet for her. Welcome this companion of the Five Great Ones to the House of Thoth, the one whom she praised and loved, the local Prince Djeheutyhotep."[37]

Here the marsh is personified in the form of a goddess. The expression *ḥb-sḫt* is used as a pun on the "catch" (*ḥb*) of the marsh and the festival (*ḥb*) of Sekhet. This catch is then transferred to Djeheutyhotep in the form of *inw n sḫt*, "*inw* of the marsh" at the west end of the north wall.

It is possible to infer that this scene represented participation in a royal ceremony, though it is by no means certain. On one hand, this scene could represent the continuation of ceremonies such as that performed by Baqet I, a ceremony of fishing or fowling that resulted directly in the conveyance of *inw* to the deceased. It would then refer to the claim of the nomarch to control *inw* derived from nature. Djeheutyhotep and his sons are then participating in a ritual of fowling that occurred independently of any other authority. On the other hand, Djeheutyhotep could be seen here as a participant in the same ceremony mentioned in the Annals of Amenemhet II. Djeheutyhotep would then be one of the officials who participated in the rewards of the catch led by the *Wḥ*ᶜ*-Nbty*, the king in the form of the Fisher/Fowler of the Two Ladies. Neither interpretation is certain.

A third nomarch who lived in early Dynasty 12, Ukhhotep II of Meir, decorated his tomb in yet another manner indicating connections to the royal authority. The texts here refer to the *inw* in the Delta marshes and all the good *inw* of the marshes that are in the Northland. These expressions differ from the *inw* of the marsh found in Khnumhotep II and Djeheutyhotep II's tombs. An even more striking difference is found in the fact that the majority of the offering bearers are female rather than male, an iconographical trait associated with royalty rather than nomarchs.

John Baines has suggested that the fecundity figures found in this tomb derive from a royal structure of the Old or Middle Kingdom.[38] This suggestion seems likely to be true, inasmuch as these figures have no obvious antecedents in Middle Kingdom provincial tombs.

Again, there are two conceivable intentions for showing this royal iconography. Ukhhotep II could be claiming a prerogative of royalty; alternatively, he could be associating himself with the emerging central power. The first explanation is often suggested.[39] Yet female offering bearers representing the royal estates are known from Memphite tombs of Dynasty 5, a time when nobles readily acknowledged their debts to the king. *Inw* is specifically mentioned in this context in the tomb of Akhethotep in Saqqara.[40] Here Ptahhotep, the son of the deceased, numbered the *inw* his father received from royal estates. Those estates, as is often the case, are personified as females. This type of scene is conceivably the source for Ukhhotep II's use of female offering bearers.

If the female offering bearers actually are intended to recall royal redistribution of *inw* to nobles, the source of the *inw* given in these inscriptions becomes clearer. It seems unlikely that Ukhhotep II could seriously claim the *inw* of the Delta independently in the manner of foreign gifts given to a king. There is no suggestion in the tomb that he claimed to be in a higher social position than the Royal House at Memphis/Itjet-tawy. It seems more likely that these scenes are actually an acknowledgment of the royal source of these gifts to Ukhhotep II. Though this is nowhere explicitly stated in words, this iconography is so unusual that it must have conveyed a clear message to contemporaries. This message could proclaim that the older interpretation of *inw* as a gift from the king had been accepted here.

Thus at the end of the provincial tomb series, it is possible to reinterpret these scenes in a "Loyalist" context: three nomarchs of early Dynasty 12 designed different ways to express their developing relationship with a newly powerful central government. Khnumhotep II acknowledged royal power through depicting a royal scribe conveying *inw* to him. Djeheutyhotep II portrayed himself participating in the fishing/fowling festival that Amenemhet II surely celebrated at Memphis. He thus depicted himself participating in the rewards of a royal gift. Finally, Ukhhotep II adopted the already ancient iconography of the female offering bearer to signal his acceptance of *inw* from the central government.

This interpretation of these scenes as an acknowledgment of royal power rather than a last attempt at local hegemony fits well with the suggestions of Eugene Cruz-Uribe and Detlef Franke. As they have argued, the generation of nobles who fully accepted Dynasty 12's authority located their tombs closer to the royal center. There was no real elimination of the nomarchs so much as an acceptance of royal power by the last generation to build tombs in the provinces and a recognition by the next generation that tombs should then be built nearer to the king. The festival that included a wrestling ritual, portrayed by Baqet I and Ukhhotep I at a time of less royal control was replaced in the three later tombs by the celebration of the hunting-fishing-fowling festival (the Heb-Sekhet?) celebrated under the leadership of the king.

Inw at the Royal Center in Dynasties 12 and 13

Dynasties 12 and 13 are particularly well documented for a discussion of *inw* at the royal center. Two archives from the royal mortuary installation of Senwosret II dating to the reigns of Senwosret III and Amenemhet III have been known to scholars since the 1890s. One group was published by Griffith in 1898 soon after its discovery by W. M. Flinders Petrie at Illahun/Kahun.[41] The second group still awaits full publication.[42] The two groups represent separate archives from the town (Petrie papyri) and from the mortuary temple (Berlin papyri). They have few points of direct contact, yet both contain references to *inw*.[43] These papyri are useful for understanding the use of *inw* at a royal mortuary temple and the attached pyramid town. To examine the actual collection and redistribution of *inw* at the royal palace itself, it is necessary to turn to P. Boulaq 18, a royal account text of Dynasty 13. Alexander Scharff's transcription is used here for transliterations.

Inw *Delivered to the Royal Palace*

27. *kmt.n.f di r pr-ᶜ3 ᶜ.w.s. m inw 1:1:1*
    That which he furnished, given to the palace l.p.h., as *inw* 1:1:1.
    Dynasty 12[44]
    Context: Cattle account from town of Illahun.

28. *in.n.f m inw ᶜḥᶜ m hrw pn*
    That which he brought, being outstanding *inw* from this day.
    Sobekhotep II[45]
    Context: Royal account papyrus.

29. *šbn ᶜḳw n nb ᶜ.w.s. n ḥ3t-sp 3 3bd 2 3ḫt (sw) 28: t šbn ᶜḳw inw*
    Various income of the Lord L.P.H. of Year 3, Month 2 of Akhet, (day) 28: Various Breads: *ᶜḳw*-bread, *inw*-bread.

Sobekhotep II[46]
Context: Royal account papyrus, headings of columns.

30. *inw ḥry n tm Ddy m wddt rdi.tw in.tw st iit m . . .*
Inw of the *ḥry n tm,* Dedy, being that which is commanded that one might cause that one might bring it. Coming with . . .
Sobekhotep II[47]
Context: Royal account papyrus.

31. *sḥwy inw hrw pn dndn st sr mnwt sn-nṯr t-ḥḏ inw imy-r niwt ṯ3ty imy-r ḥwt wrt 6 ʿnḫw*
Assemblage of the *inw* of this day: *dndn*-fowl, pintail ducks, geese, pigeons, incense, white bread: *inw* of the mayor, vizier, overseer of the six great law domains, Ankhu.
Sobekhotep II[48]
Context: Royal account text, a list of individuals who gave *inw* to the king.

32. *in.n.f m inw ḥ3 tp n [. . .]*
That which he brought as *inw* of the department of [. . .].
Sobekhotep II[49]
Context: Royal account papyrus, part of a list of "various income."

33. *sḥwy inw n hrw pn kmt wʿrt tp rsy ḫ3 pr n dd rmṭ*
Assemblage of *inw* for this day. Delivered (from): Department of the the Head of the South, Labor Bureau (?).
Sobekhotep II[50]
Context: Royal account papyrus.

34. *inw [ḫ3] dd rmṯ*
Inw of the Labor Bureau (?).
Sobekhotep II[51]
Context: Royal account papyrus, heading.

35. *inw wꜥrt tp rsy ḥrt-ꜥ*

Inw of the Department of the Head of the South: arrears.

Sobekhotep II[52]

Context: List of arrears from various individuals in a royal account papyrus.

The archives from Illahun dating to the reigns of Senwosret III through Amenemhet III and Papyrus Boulaq 18 from Dynasty 13 reveal an unusual amount of concrete detail about sending *inw* to the royal palace.

One example from the town of Illahun shows that individuals from this installation paid *inw* to the living king in the palace. In this text, the transaction is viewed simply, with no recognition of the complicated bureaucratic structure that was actually involved.

By the reign of Senwosret III, new government administrative departments had been established that dealt with conveying *inw* to the royal centers.[53] These were known as *wꜥrt tp-rsy*, "The Sector of the Head of the South," *ẖ3 n dd rmṯ*, generally understood to be the "Labor Bureau," and *pr-ḥḏ*, "The Treasury."[54] As these examples show, the Department of the Head of the South and the Labor Bureau are the two authorities specifically credited with supplying *inw* to the palace.

Very often the *inw* listed in these examples is credited to an individual. This implies that part of the definition of *inw* as a technical accounting term was a gift from an individual to the king in the reign of Sobekhotep II. This information must be taken seriously when it is drawn from account texts rather than tomb or temple walls. As Stephen Quirke has commented, these texts provide information with "the minimum distortion from subjective interpolators."[55] In this case, this information supports observations made about *inw* in other periods when the central government was in operation.

Inw ***Redistributed at the Royal Center***

Inw Ḥbyt ***at a Royal Mortuary Temple***

36. *ḥ3t-sp 14 3bd 4 3ḫt sw 24 m3ʿt r Sḫm-Snwsrt-m3ʿ-ḫrw m ḥbyt nt Skr n Nsw-Bity Ḫʿ- ḫpr-rʿ . . . inw ḥ3ty-ʿ [. . .] m ḥby nt Ḥb Skr*

Regnal Year 14, Month 4 of Akhet, Day 24: Offering to (the temple of) Sekhem-Senwosret-Justified, being the festival offerings of the Sokar (festival) belonging to the King of Upper and Lower Egypt Khakheperre [Senwosret II] . . . *Inw* of the Mayor [. . .] being a festival offering of the Festival of Sokar.

Senwosret III/Amenemhet III[56]

Context: Income of royal mortuary temple during Sokar Festival.

37. *ḥ3t-sp 14 3bd 4 3ḫt sw 24 m3ʿt r Sḫm-Snwsrt-m3ʿ-ḫrw m ḥbyt nt Skr n nsw-bity Ḫʿ- ḫpr-rʿ iw3 sip ḫry iw3 Ḫnt-ḥtp ḥ3t-sp 10 + x (14 ?) [. . .] inw ḥ3ty-ʿ [. . .] m ḥbyt nt ḥb skr . . .*

Year 14, Month 4 of Akhet, Day 24: Offering to [the temple of] Sekhem-Senwosret-Justified, being the festival offerings of Sokar for the King of Upper and Lower Egypt Khakheperre: oxen, being inspected by the Overseer of Cattle, Khent-hotep. Year 14 (?) [. . .] *inw* of the Mayor [. . .] being the festival offerings of the Festival of Sokar . . .

Senwosret III/Amenemhet III[57]

Context: Income of royal mortuary temple during the Sokar Festival.

38. *ḥ3t-sp 9 tp 3ḫt sw 26 inw ḥbyt nt ḥm-k3 n ḥmt-nsw*

Regnal Year 9, First month of Akhet, Day 26: Festival offerings of the soul-priest of the Queen [. . .].

Amenemhet III[58]

Context: Offering list for the temple of Anubis.

39. *inw ḥbyt nt ḥm-k3 ḥmt-nsw ẖnmt-nfr*
Inw of the festival offerings belonging to the soul priest of the Queen, Khnumet-nefer.
Senwosret III/Amenemhet III[59]
Context: Daily entry of festival offerings (I Akhet 27).

40. *inw ḥbyt irt n mty-s3w ʿḥʿ.f m 3bd[.f]*
Inw of the festival offerings, that which was celebrated by the Controller of the Phyle when he arose in [his] month.
Senwosret III/Amenemhet III[60]
Context: Daily income entry (IV Shomu 8).

41. *. . . sw 22 . . . in[w] ḥbyt nt mty n s3 [S-n]-wsr[t . . .]*
. . . Day 22 . . . *in[w]* of the festival offerings of the Controller of the Phyle of [Sen]wosre[t] . . .
Reign of Senwosret III/Amenemhet III[61]
Context: Daily income entry.

42. *ḥ3t-sp 32 3bd 3 3ẖt sw 6 iwḥ inw ḥbyt nt [. . .] . . . inw ḥbyt nt mty s3w s3-b3stt s3 spy . . . ḥ3t-sp 32 3bd 3 3ẖt sw 7 iwḥ mnṯw-ḥtp s3 mnw-ḥtp ir hrw n 3bd r inw inw ḥbyt nt hrw pn . . . inw ḥbyt nt mty-s3 s3-b3stt s3 spy . . . ḫsb ʿḳw ḥbyt nt mty-s3w s3-b3stt s3 spy*
Regnal Year 32, Month 3 of Akhet, Day 6 of the Inundation: *Inw* of the Festival of [. . .] . . . *Inw* of the Festival of the Controller of Phyles, Si-Bastet's son Sepy . . . Regnal Year 32, Month 3 of Akhet, Day 7 of the Inundation: Mentuhotep's son Minhotep, making (?) a day of the month for *inw, inw* of the festival offerings of this day . . . *inw* of the festival offerings of the Controller of the Phyle, Si-Bastet's son Sepy . . . reckoning of the provisions of the the festival offerings of the Controller of the Phyle, Se-Bastet's son Sepy.
Senwosret III/Amenemhet III[62]

Context: Temple daybook, ration list for the phyle. Final (monthly) reckoning of the phyle leader.

43. *inw ḥbyt nt rnpt nt s3-nsw [Sn]-wsr[t-snb] inw wʿrt mḥtt ẖrp ḥr Ḥtp-[Sn-]wsrt[-m3ʿ- ḫrw] in.n imy-r šnʿ n ḥptw-nṯr Rn.f-w3ḥ s3 Sbk-nḫt*

Inw of the Festival offerings of the year of the Prince Senwosret-seneb. *Inw* of the Department of the North, being conducted from (?) (the town of) Hetep-Senwosret-Justified, which was brought by the Overseer of the Granary of Divine Offerings, Renef-wakh's son Sobek-nakht.

Amenemhet III/Senwosret III[63]

Context: Temple daybook, income of bread, beer flour, and list of individuals.

44. *[ḥ3t-sp 5 3bd 2 prt] sw 25 iwḥ [. . .] ḥ3t sp 5 3bd 2 sw 27 iwḥ mnw-ḥtp s3 S-n-wsrt-[. . .] m3ʿ.n nsw-bity [. . .] m3ʿ-ḫrw m ḥbyt nt [. . .] in.n imy s3 n[. . .] mny . . . inw ḥbyt nt hrw pn . . . inw mty s3 imy 3bd.f*

[Regnal Year 5, Month 2 of Peret,] Day 25 of Inundation: [. . .] Regnal Year 5, Month 2 of Peret, Day 27 of Inundation: Min-hotep's son Senwosret-[. . .]. That which the King of Upper and Lower Egypt [. . .], justified, offered as a festival offering belonging to [. . .] which the Overseer of the Phyle of [. . .], Meny, brought. *Inw* of the festival offerings belonging to this day. *Inw* of the Controller of the Phyle who is in his month.

Senwosret III/Amenemhet III[64]

Context: Temple daybook, daily entries and monthly inventory.

45. *inw ḥbyt nt sšwt [. . .] pn ḥmt-nsw ẖnmt-nfr [. . .] . . . inw ḥ3ty-ʿ [. . .] in.n imy-r nt (sic) [. . .] m hrw pn [. . .] inw mty s3w snby s3 spy-m-[. . .] in.n sš ḥnw*

Inw of the Festival offerings of (?) this [. . .] of the Queen Khnumet-nefer [. . .] . . . *inw* of the Mayor [. . .] which the Overseer of (?) brought [. . .] on this day [. . .] *inw* of the Controller of Phyles Senbi's son Sepy-em-? which the scribe Henou brought.

Senwosret III/Amenemhet III[65]

Context: Delivery of offerings.

Ursula Kaplony-Heckel, the scholar who has most recently published descriptions of these papyri, understood them for the most part to be lists of temple income. Using the traditional model of *inw,* the mortuary temple of Senwosret II received this kind of gift from a variety of sources. As was the case at the royal mortuary temple of Neferirkare at Abu Sir in the Old Kingdom, the royal connections of the temple allowed some goods destined for its use to be considered possessions of the deceased king; it was therefore *inw.* The local Princes (*ḥ3ty-ʿ*) are among those who deliver these gifts (P. Berlin 10,041r). Various other officials, such as the Soul Priest of the Queen and Phyle Controllers, also contribute (P. Berlin 10,044e; 10,045c; 10,045a). In one case the neighboring town and even the living king contribute *inw* to the mortuary temple (P. Berlin 10,009r).

The same *inw ḥbyt* is redistributed by the temple to the phyles that perform rituals there (P. Berlin 10,006). Here it is clear that *inw* has a broad range of meaning referring to gifts to the mortuary temple from the king, and a variety of other people on the one hand, and gifts given as rations to phyle members.

Festival *inw* can be collected or distributed regardless of whether it is a festival day. Only two texts from this group explicitly refer to a festival as the occasion for exchanging *inw.* This text is dated during the Festival of Sokar and appears to contain references to goods used as part of its celebration. It does not seem impossible, however, that festival *inw* comes to the mortuary temple under circumstances similar to those seen in the tombs of great nobles of the Old Kingdom and nomarchs of Dynasties 11 and 12. Perhaps these texts record actual delivery of goods that are somehow pledged officially to the mortuary temple during a festival or certain festivals.

Inw ḥtp-nṯr

46. ***sḥwy n sšmw inw ḥwt-nṯr nt*** *Inpw tpy ḏw.f m Sḫm-Snwsrt-m3c-ḫrw s3ᶜ n ḥ3t-sp 1 3bd 3 prt sw 1 nfryt ḥ3t-sp 2 3bd 2 prt ᶜrḳy r-ḫt [ḥtpw]-nṯr [. . .] ḥ3t-[sp] 1 inw ḥtpw-nṯr [. . .] inw ḥwt-nṯr [nsw-bi]ty Ḫᶜ-ḫpr-rᶜ m3ᶜ-ḫrw m Sḫm-Snwsrt m3c-ḫrw inw ḥtpw-nṯr [. . .] wḏ3.tw Sbḳ-Š m ḥ3t-sp 2 3bd 3 inw ḥtpw-nṯr [. . .] Ḫnw m ḥ3t-sp 2 3bd 3 inw [. . .] dmḏ [. . .]*

Summary of expenditures (conducting) of inw of the temple of Anubis-on-his-Mountain-in-Sekhem-Senwosret-Justified from Year 1, Month 3 of Peret, Day 1 to Year 2 Month 2 of Peret, last day of the month. List of *[ḥtpw-]nṯr*-offerings [. . .] (of ?) Year 1, *inw* of the *ḥtp-nṯr*-offerings [. . .] *inw* of the Temple of [The King of Upper and Lower Egypt] Khakheperre-Justified in Sekhem-Senwosret-Justified. *Inw* of the *ḥtpw-nṯr* offerings [. . .] that proceeded [from?] Sobek-She in Year 2 Month 3, *inw* of the *ḥtpw-nṯr*-offerings [. . .] (of ?) the Residence in Year 2 Month 3, *inw* of . . . Total . . .

Senwosret III/Amenemhet III[66]

Context: Temple daybook, list of temple expenditures.

47. ***inw r-ḫt h3b.tw r Mry-sbḳ*** *in.n . . . Inpw swḏ3-ib pw n nb.i ᶜ.w.s. ḥr p3 ḥtpw-nṯr m3ᶜ.n nsw-bity Ḫᶜ-ḫpr-rᶜ m3ᶜ-ḫrw innw m ḥwt-nṯr Sbḳ Šdt innt.tw n.k iw b3k im ḥr h3b ḥr sp ᶜš3 nfr pw dr.tw sdb im*

Inw: list of what was sent to Mery-Sobek, that which [. . . ?]-anubis brought: It is a communication for My Lord, l.p.h., concerning the *ḥtp-nṯr*-offerings which the King of Upper and Lower Egypt, Khakheperre, justified, offered and what is brought from the temple of Sobek of the Lake. As for that which is brought to you, your humble servant sent at many times (to say), “It is good.” May one drive out impediments thereto.

Senwosret III/Amenemhet III[67]
Context: A letter copied into the Temple daybook.

48. *inw n mdt n iḥwt . . . inw mdt nt ḥtpw-nṯr*
inw of the stalled cattle of cattle offering . . . *inw* of the stalled cattle belonging to the *ḥtp- nṯr* offering.
Senwosret III/Amenemhet III[68]
Context: Temple daybook: summary of offerings for the Temple of Anubis on the Mountain in Sekhem-Senwosret-Justified.

These two texts attest to the exceedingly complicated relationships among various institutions that both received and disbursed *inw*. P. Berlin 10,007 describes disbursements from the Temple of Anubis within the precinct of the mortuary temple of Senwosret II to the main temple, to the temple of Sobek of the Lake, and to the Residence. P. Berlin 10,056A refers to a disbursement from the main cult center to a certain Mery-Sobek, who may represent an institution. In this case, the gift is conceived by the writer as originating with the deceased king, Senwosret II. It is not at all clear whether the model that describes a gift exchange between socially unequal parties is represented here. First, the exchanges are made between institutions rather than individuals. Second, there is no external evidence that would indicate that there is some sort of recognized hierarchy among different kinds of temple establishments. Perhaps these texts represent a sharing or reversion of offerings among equals. But even this solution is not altogether satisfying, because the meaning of *inw* is further blurred if it is true. A final suggestion might be that once *inw* became the property of a temple, its disbursement no longer was governed by the same restrictions that are found in regard to *inw* under the control of an individual.

Inw Ḥtp-S-n-wsrt

49. *inw Ḥtp-S-n-wsrt-m3ᶜ-ḫrw inn [. . . m3ᶜ n (?)] nsw-bity Ḫᶜ-ḫpr-rᶜ m3ᶜ-ḫrw*

Inw of (the town of) Hetep-Senwosret-Justified which [PN? . . .] brought [which was offered to (?)] the king of Upper and Lower Egypt Khakheperre, justified.
Senwosret III/Amenemhet III[69]
Context: Temple daybook, list of offerings.

50. *ḥ3t-sp 33 3bd 3 šmw [sw 20 + x . . .] inw Ḥtp-S-n-wsrt-m3ᶜ-ḫrw in.n [. . .]*
Regnal Year 33, Month 3 of Shomu, Day 20 + x: *Inw* of [the town of] Hetep-Senwosret-Justified which PN (?) brought. . . .
Senwosret III/Amenemhet III[70]
Context: Temple daybook, list of offerings.

51. *inw n wᶜrt mḥtt*
Inw of the Northern sector [of the town ?].
Senwosret III/Amenemhet III[71]
Context: Temple daybook, deliveries to the mortuary temple, Kahun.

52. *ḥ3t-sp 2 3bd 4(-nw n) prt sw 10 (+x) inw b3kw sb3w*
Regnal Year 2, month 4 of Peret, day 10 (+x), *inw* and *b3kw* of the teacher.
Dynasty 12[72]
Context: Town at Illahun.

53. *ḥ3t-sp 10(?) 3bd 4(-nw n) šmw sw 3 inw ḫtmty bity smr wᶜty imy-r3 ḫtmtyw Sn-wsrt m(?) inw wḥmw n ᶜrryt Ḫw-nfri inw tsw Ḫty-ᶜnḫ . . .*
Year 10(?), month 4 of summer, day 3, *inw* of the Royal Seal Bearer, Sole Friend and Overseer of the Seal Bearers, Senwoseret, consisting of(?) *inw* of the Herald of the Judgment Hall, Hounefery, *inw* of the commander, Khetyankh. . . .
Dynasty 12[73]
Context: Town of Illahun.

54. *ḥ3t-sp 38 3bd 4 3ḫt sw 16 r-ḫt krhwt nty (sic) r irt r inw*
Regnal Year 38, Month 4 of Inundation, Day 16, list of vessels that will be made for *inw*.
Dynasty 12[74] (Amenemhet III ?)
Context: Kahun papyri.

The town of Hetep-Senwosret was to some extent a supporter of the temple of Sekhem-Senwosret through gifts called *inw*. This circulation of goods represented by gifts from the town to the temple and gifts redistributed to the phyle members, who must have been residents of the town, as rations, is a perfect representation in microcosm of the Egyptian economy. The fact that this exchange is called *inw* must depend on the identity of the deity of this temple. Even in death, gifts to a king are called *inw* when donated by a variety of individuals. Gifts from this source are also called *inw*.

Inw ***to Support the Royal Family***

55. ***kt wpt iit.n sr p[n] ḥr[.s]*** *i[mi f3i.tw] gs n p3 [k3] n [ḥmt] n[swt] [ᶜ.w.s.] ḥnᶜ rdit f3i.tw n n3-n srw [rmṯ] n pr mnᶜ[wt] snwt-n[sw] m p3 inw [m hrw pn] ir ḫft wpwt tn*
Another commission concerning which this magistrate came. Cau[se that one carry] a side of beef to the Qu[een l.p.h.] together with the causing that one carry to the magistrates, the people of the house of the nur[ses], and the [roy]al sisters, from the *inw* [of this day]. Done according to this commission.
Sobekhotep II[75]
Context: Royal account text.

56. *šd m ḫ[t]m di r k3p r inw n ḥmt-nsw ᶜ.w.s.*
"Removed from the keep, given to the nursery to be *inw* of the Queen, l.p.h."
Sobekhotep II[76]
Context: Royal account text.

57. *inw imy-r [ẖnr?] . . . ḥmt-nsw ᶜ.w.s. ḥ[m]3t r pr ḥmt-nsw Iy ᶜ.w.s.*
Inw of the Overseer of the [Harim?] . . . of(?) the Queen, L.P.H., salt for the palace of Queen Iy, l.p.h.
Sobekhotep II[77]
Context: Royal account papyrus.

58. ***iit n imy-r ᶜẖnwty n k3p Rn.f-m-ib ḥr.s m prt iw.n.f ḥr.s*** *imi f3i.tw n ḥmt-nsw Snwt-nsw snw-nsw msw-nsw ᶜ.w.s. m n3-n inw n hrw pn ir ẖft wpwt tn*
Coming of the Chamberlain of the Nursery Renefemib concerning it, going forth, after he came about it. Cause that one carry to the Queen, the royal sisters, the royal brothers, and the royal children from the *inw* of this day. Done according to this commission.
Sobekhotep II[78]
Context: Royal account papyrus.

59. *inw imy-r ᶜẖnwty k3p Kky kmt n Nw*
"*Inw* of the Overseer of the Chamberlain of the Nursery, Keky. That which was provided to Nu."
Sobekhotep III[79]
Context: Royal account papyrus.

Examples of *inw* redistribution found in P. Boulaq 18 attest to its importance as a means of supporting the royal family. It is this aspect of *inw* that most clearly identifies it as an element of the royal privy-purse. In addition to using *inw* to cement the loyalties of various constituencies throughout Egypt, the king also used *inw* to provide for the harim and nursery.

Quirke has correctly stressed that the use of *inw* at the palace was a special delivery rather than a regular means of support.[80] It was often called into use for a major distribution of food outside of ordinary expenses. This point has also been stressed by Anthony Spalinger.[81] He has pointed out the *inw* columns were included in this document when additional special payments had to be made to state officials. *Inw* was not the only or even the major source of royal support. Its importance as something separate from ordinary income is clear in these accounts as well as the way it was portrayed in tomb scenes and in other festival settings.

Excursus on *Inw* as Products in Literature

All of the following examples are drawn from literary texts of the Middle Kingdom. It is not possible to assign more specific dates to them.

60. *ʿḥʿ.n ʿḳ.kwi ḥr Ity ms.n.i n.f inw pn in.n.i m-ẖnw n iw pn*
Then I entered to the Sovereign and I presented to him this *inw* which I had brought from the interior of this island.
Middle Kingdom[82]
Context: *The Story of the Shipwrecked Sailor.*

61. *iw grg.tw n.i iw w3ḥ.t(w) n.i ḥrw-r inw n ṯsmw.i*
One hunted for me. One laid down for me in addition to the *inw* of my hounds.
Dynasty 12[83]
Context: *Story of Sinuhe.*

62. *n ms ḫd.tw r [kp]ny min ptr irt.n r ʿšw n sʿḥ.n ḳrs.tw wʿb[w] m inw.sn sdwḫ [wr]w m sfṯ iry r-mn-m kftyw n ii.n.sn*
Indeed, no one sails northward to [By]blos today. What shall we do concerning pinetrees for our mummies? It is with their *inw* that priests are buried. It is with the oil thereof that nobles as far as Crete are embalmed. They cannot come.
Dynasty 12[84]
Context: *Admonitions of an Egyptian Sage.*

63. *h3t pw ir.n sḫty pn r kmt 3tp.n.f ʿ3w.f m i33w rdmt etc. m inw nb nfr n sḫt ḥm3t*
This peasant went down to Egypt, he having loaded his

donkeys with rushes, *rdmt*-grass, etc. being all the good *inw* of the Wadi Natrun.

Dynasty 12[85]

Context: *The Eloquent Peasant.*

In two cases, *The Shipwrecked Sailor* and *The Story of Sinuhe,* the author may be referring to the technical accounting term *inw* as a gift exchanged between a king and a person of lesser social position. The examples from the *Admonitions* and the *Eloquent Peasant,* however, surely must be understood simply as "products." This bifurcation of meaning for the term must have grown out of the confusion apparent in provincial tombs decorated in the period of gradual acceptance of the authority of the central government by the nomarchs. Though this dual meaning of *inw* must be recognized in Middle Kingdom texts, it is not the intended meaning in texts describing *inw* as it is used at the palace or in exchanges between the king and others.

Conclusions about *Inw* in the First Intermediate Period and the Middle Kingdom

The First Intermediate Period and the Middle Kingdom preserve a much larger and more varied body of evidence for a discussion of *inw* than did the Archaic Period and Old Kingdom. A summary of the evidence can now be presented along with an analysis of the meaning of *inw* during this period.

The contraction and virtual disappearance of the central government at the end of the Old Kingdom meant that local rulers assumed responsibility for collecting and disbursing *inw* in the First Intermediate Period. By the end of Dynasty 11, local authorities had devised at least two occasions for the collection of *inw.* These occasions were two kinds of festivals. The first festival shared some of the characteristics of the Thoth Festival depicted in the tomb of Ptahhotep II at Saqqara. The second festival during which *inw* was collected was a nature festival related to fowling and fishing in the marshes. This festival has much less clear Old Kingdom antecedents and may have been a provincial innovation. Whether the nature festival was an innovation, it continued to be practiced at Memphis by the king during the reign of Amenemhet II.

The kings of Dynasty 11 restored traditional Old Kingdom ideas about *inw* collection, at least in Upper Egypt. Evidence from provincial tombs in Middle Egypt including Beni Hasan, Bersheh, and Meir indicate that local rulers there continued to collect *inw* for their own use until the time of Senwosret II. Tomb paintings in these three areas do reveal a gradual acceptance of royal authority in their handling of scenes of collecting *inw*. No standardization was established for this genre of scene before the abandonment of local provincial tombs by these families. Presumably, rising provincial families established tombs associated with royal mortuary establishments after this period.

The importance of *inw* at royal mortuary establishments can be seen at Kahun/Illahun, both in the archives of the temples and of the pyramid town. *Inw* is important for the support of the mortuary temple, the local Temple of Anubis, and for the support of residents of the pyramid town. The archives depict a microcosm of the Egyptian economy. There was mutual exchange between temple and town with some assistance from the Residence.

Finally, P. Boulaq 18 reveals the way in which *inw* was used on reaching the royal palace. There it supported the royal family and helped meet unexpected expenses.

The picture of *inw* emerging from the Middle Kingdom is much more varied than was true of the Archaic Period and Old Kingdom. A notable difference in the later periods is the continuation of the term in the absence of royal authority. This continuation led to some blurring of the technical meaning of the term, especially when it was used to mean "products" in literary texts. That the technical term was never forgotten is very clear in the bureaucratic texts from Illahun and in P. Boulaq 18.

The question remains whether this variation was a historical development resulting from new usage of the word or whether the more limited evidence available from the earlier period also inhibits a true understanding of the term in the Old Kingdom. This question is best reserved for the final conclusions in chapter 5. Chapter 4 will show how *inw* once again expanded its meaning in the changing political circumstances of the New Kingdom.

Chapter Four

Inw *in the New Kingdom: The View from Monumental Inscriptions*

Evidence from the New Kingdom reveals aspects of *inw* not obvious in the sources preserved from earlier periods in Egyptian history. The large number of inscribed royal monuments, including both mortuary temples and temples of the gods, record the official view of *inw.* In this period of strong central government the evidence describes the centrality of the king's role in *inw* collection and disbursement. Furthermore, the texts disclose an emphasis on the personal dimension in exchanges of *inw* during the New Kingdom. Finally, the evidence from the New Kingdom expands our knowledge of the uses made of *inw* by the king and its administration in Thebes.

Inw as the Royal Privy-Purse

Three observations support the proposition that *inw* in the New Kingdom represents contributions to the king's privy-purse. The first is that *inw* was considered an aspect of kingship, aside from the general idea that the king owned everything in the world. Second, the texts stress that *inw* was delivered directly to the king or his official representative. Finally, it is clear that the king redistributes *inw* for specific royal purposes rather than as part of the wider redistributive system.

Inw *as an Aspect of Kingship*

The first observation indicating that *inw* was the king's personal property is found in the explicit promises made to various kings by the gods. In these cases, possession of *inw* was part of a catalog of royal attributes.

1. *sn.ṯ ḏ3ḏ3.w n.w mšꜥ.w ꜥm.ṯ wr.w n.w Rtnw ẖr šꜥt sp nw (i)t(f).f inw.t m s . . .*
   May you sever the heads of soldiers, may you grasp (read *3mm*) the Chiefs of Retenu, possessing the terror of the time of your father, your *inw* consisting of men . . .
   Hatshepsut[1]
   Context: The gods speak to Hatshepsut on her Northern journey. Deir el Bahri.

2. *inw ꜥ3 n ḫ3st*
   The great *inw* of the foreign country.
   Thutmose IV[2]
   Context: Among things promised to the king by Reharakhty. Sphinx Stela.

3. *di.i ḥr.i r rsy bi3y.i n.k di.i pẖr n.k wr.w kš ḫst ẖr inw.sn nb.w ḥr psd.sn di.i ḥr.i r mḥty bi3.i n.k di.(i) iwt n.k ḫ3swt pḥw Stt ẖr inw.sn nbw ḥr psd.sn*
   I turn my face southward that I might perform a miracle for you. I cause that the princes of wretched Kush might travel to you bearing all their *inw* on their backs. I turn my face northward that I might perform a miracle for you. I cause that the foreign countries of the ends of Asia might come to you bearing all their *inw* on their backs.
   Amenhotep III[3]

Context: A speech of Amun to the king. Stela in his mortuary temple.

4. *di.i iw n.k wr.w ḫ3s.wt rsy.w di.sn šsp.k inw*
   I cause that the chiefs of the southern foreign countries might come to you that they might cause that you might receive *inw.*
   Sety I[4]
   Context: Amun speaks to the king. Karnak Temple.

5. *imi nḫt ḫpš.f r t3.w nb.w iw.w n šfyt.f ḫr inw.sn*
   Cause that his sword might triumph in every land that they might come to his majesty bearing their *inw.*
   Ramesses III[5]
   Context: The king requests these thing of the gods for his son.

In all of these cases, *inw* was conceived as a result of divine intervention for the king. The fact that these deliveries from foreign lands were to the king rather than an institution or Egypt as a geographical or political entity was stressed.

Evidence for Inw *as the Royal Privy-Purse*

The king almost always received the *inw* personally or through a representative who had the authority to act on the king's behalf. This contrasts with other forms of commodity exchange.[6] The following examples illustrate this point.

6. *iṯt.n.i rnp.wt ꜥš3.wt m ḥ3ty-ꜥ n Nḫn ms.n.i inw.s n nb t3.wy*
   I spent many years as Mayor of Hierakonopolis, I having presented its *inw* to the Lord of the Two Lands.
   Early Dyn. 18[7]
   Context: Stela of Hor-meni (Florence 2549).

7. "The Southerners come downstream, the Northerners

come upstream," *ḫ3swt nbwt dmd.w ẖr inw.sn n nṯr nfr sp tpy ꜥ3-ḫpr-k3-rꜥ ꜥnḫ dt*

All the foreign countries being gathered together bearing their *inw* for the Good God of the first occasion, Aakhperkare, living forever.

Thutmose I[8]

Context: Royal inscription at Tombos.

8. "The Nine Bows are gathered under his sandals," *iw n.f Mntyw ẖr inw*

   The Mentyu-Asiatics come to him [the King] bearing their *inw.*

   Thutmose II[9]

   Context: Royal inscription located between Aswan and Philae.

9. *šsp inw n wr n Pwnt in wpwty-nsw*

   Receiving the *inw* of the Prince of Punt by the Royal Messenger.

   Hatshepsut[10]

   Context: Punt reliefs from Mortuary Temple of the Queen. Deir el Bahri.

10. "Then this enemy and the Princes who were with him caused that their children be brought forth with them," *ẖr inw ꜥš3 m nbw ḥr ḥḏ . . . ꜥḥꜥ.n in.n.sn st m inw n ḥm.i*

    Bearing great amounts of *inw* consisting of gold and silver. . . . Now they brought it as *inw* of My Majesty.

    Thutmose III[11]

    Context: Annals of Thutmose III. Karnak Temple.

11. *iw n.f wr.w Mtn inw.sn ḥr psḏ.w.sn r dbḥ ḥtp.w ḥm.f sb.tw ṯ3w.f nḏm n ꜥnḫ*

    The Princes of Mittani come to him with their *inw* on their backs in order to request the peace of His Majesty and that his sweet breath of life be sent.

Amenhotep II[12]
Context: Inscription on columns between pylons IV and V, Karnak Temple.

12. *wr.w Nhrn ẖr inw.sn gmḥ.sn Mn-ḫpr.w-rᶜ wḏ3.f m pr.f sḏm.sn ḫrw.f mi s3 Nt*
The Chiefs of Naharain bear their *inw* that they might behold Menkheperure when he proceeds from his house and that they might hear his voice like the Son of Nut.
Thutmose IV[13]
Context: Historical scarab.

13. *t3.w nb.w ḫ3s.wt nb.wt ẖr inw.sn . . . ḫrp.sn n k3 nḫt Ḥr ḫᶜ m m3ᶜt . . . Nb-m3ᶜt-rᶜ*
Every land and every foreign country bears its *inw.* They conduct (it) to the Strong Bull, Horus Who-Appears-in-Truth, etc. . . . Nebmaatre.
Amenhotep III[14]
Context: Architrave inscription, Luxor Temple.

Several formulas are used to describe the delivery of *inw* to the king. The outstanding fact is that it is delivered most often to the king in person. Secondarily it can be received by his representative such as the vizier or a royal messenger. The following table is a breakdown of the formulas that indicate to whom the *inw* is brought.

Table of Recipients of Inw

To the King personally:		
1. *n nb t3.wy*	to the Lord of the Two Lands	*Urk.* IV, 76:15–16.
2. *n nsw*	to the King	*Urk.* IV, 77:7–9.
3. *n* King's Name	to King P.N.	*Urk.* IV, 83:9–10; 1693:8–12.
4. *r bw ḥr ḥm.f*	to the place where H.M. is	*Urk.* IV, 331:8–10; 1097:7–16.

5. *n b3.w ḥm.f*	to the powers of H.M.	*Urk.* IV, 662:14–16; 671:6; 689:17; 717:8; 726:13–14; 809:8–10; 896:15–16; 951:4–14; 1098:14–1099:5; 1094:6–14.
6. *n ḥm.f* or *ḥm.k*	to His Majesty or Your Majesty	*Urk.* IV, 688:4; 688:3; 699:4; 950:9–10.
To a King's Representative:		
7. *šsp inw n* Place Name *in* Official	receiving the *inw* of . . . by . . .	*Urk.* IV, 326:2–3 (messenger); 523:5–6 (vizier); 512:13 (vizier).
8. *m3 inw n* Place *in* Official	viewing the *inw* of . . . by . . .	*Urk.* IV, 953:13–14; 153:16 (both vizier).

Although this table shows that the king received *inw* under different names, in all cases where the text indicates for whom the *inw* was intended, that person was the king.

Considered alone, this is not a particularly surprising conclusion. It is something of an Egyptological cliche that the king owns everything. This universal claim, though it justifies the king's right in theory to take possession of goods, does not explain the mechanics of how the economy worked in practice. Commodities must have been collected and allocated according to an orderly system to enable a large bureaucracy to function. That such a system did exist is clear in the Annals of Thutmose III. The scribe of the Annals was always careful to assign any goods collected in West Asia and Nubia to a specific category. The simple formula always starts with *r-ḫt n,* "list of," followed by the category such as *inw, b3k.t ḥ3ḳ, kfᶜ*, and so forth. That such distinctions were made demonstrates that some accounting principle was being applied. Because the nature of the goods themselves did not affect its category, it seems likely that these words represent a group of objects intended for a specific end. Words like *ḥ3ḳ* and *kfᶜ* additionally indicate that the goods were obtained by military activity. *Inw,* however, was paid on a yearly basis directly to the king by conquered and independent foreigners as well as Egyptians. This personal exchange between the king and other individuals reveals the essentially social nature of these exchanges. The exchange of *inw* stood in direct contrast to the exchange of *b3k.t* which was always paid by a country or a region. Thus *inw* represented the results or cementing of a personal relationship between the king and a chief of a particular area.

The Egyptian king clearly did not believe this exchange was occurring between equals. The texts and reliefs depicting these transactions always showed the giver as subservient to the king. Exchanges of *inw* were always made "with bowed head" or "with bowing" on the part of the giver. Yet acknowledgment of social inferiority, as in the case of the Keftiu *inw* bearers, does not indicate necessarily an attempt to propagandize concerning Keftiu's dependence on Egypt. These phrases more likely referred to standard court procedure. It is safe to assume that no one ever approached the king without the appropriate ritual gestures. Though these rituals are not understood in detail, it is clear that they must have been strictly observed by foreign princes and their ambassadors as well as Egyptians. But observance of Egyptian court ritual cannot be taken as evidence for a claim of political subjugation. It is only the misunderstanding of *inw* that led to such an interpretation in the first place. *Inw* then can be defined from the foregoing observations in the following way. It was first the god-given right of the king to receive *inw*. It was an exchange where princes gave commodities to the king regardless of actual political domination. In theory, if not always in practice, it was conceived as a face-to-face exchange where goods were offered to the king in exchange for the "breath of life."[15] It occurs on a yearly basis, but the goods received are carefully separated from other collections of goods. Such a complex of concepts is most easily explained as a gift.[16]

Gift-giving is well attested worldwide as a means of exchange.[17] It has been studied by anthropologists in North American, South Pacific, African, and ancient Near Eastern cultures. In general, gift-giving is governed by conventions concerning what goods qualify as gifts and who can participate in the process based on social status or kinship. Gifts are defined by social obligations rather than economic criteria. The giving of a gift strengthens and cements a social relationship and requires an affirmation of a participant's place in a social hierarchy.

Gift-giving, then, cannot be confused with trade. The purpose of gift-giving is social whereas trade does not encompass any social obligation. C. Daryll Forde and Mary Douglas have aptly distinguished the two phenomena. They differentiate gifts and trade by observing that a gift exchange establishes or strengthens a social relationship, whereas trade assumes that any continuous relationship between the parties is incidental. Nonindustrial economies occasionally have elements of commercial trade practiced in them, but they often have developed systems of exchange through gifts that "distribute supplies at the same time as they cement social relationships."[18] The lines between social and political relationships in ancient Egyptian thought were not clearly distinguished. The king had the same social relationship, that is, a relationship expressed by *inw*-exchange, with the conquered prince of a West Asian city-state, the independent king of Babylonia, and the princes of Punt and Crete. He was in a *inw*-exchanging relationship with all of these foreign potentates as well as the inhabitants of the Two Lands. Yet this relationship could not have been conceived as indicative of political domination. An examination of exchanges of *inw* in relation to conquest in Thutmose III's Annals is instructive.

Megiddo was clearly one of the towns conquered by Thutmose III. The description of the conquest in the Annals does not include exchange of *inw,* though it was included in the Gebel Barkal account.[19] The version given in the Annals views *ḥ*^{c}*ḳ* and *kf*^{c}, "plunder" and "booty," as the result of the defeat and capitulation of the princes.[20] The grain tax is also given with their surrender. Likewise, *In-r-t,* Naharain, *In-iw-ks,* and Tunip were plundered without giving *inw* to the king.[21] *Inw* was collected from other conquered areas such as Retenu and Wartjet but was conveyed by independent areas such as Assyria, Genbut, Sengar, and Hatti.[22] *Inw*-exchanges did occur after military conquests, but this was more a sign of a return to normal relations at the end of a war. Clearly, then, the degree of hegemony the king exercised over an area did not dictate whether or not that area offered *inw*.

The true meaning of *inw* becomes increasingly more elusive to the modern observer as the familiar concepts of trade and tribute are eliminated as explanations for it. This is because such behavior seems irrational to the modern mind. Yet within the social context of the ancient Near East, such behavior was not only rational, but also an expected response to a given social situation. Foreign relations for ancient Near Eastern rulers were based on a social hierarchy and on personal relationships of one ruler to another within that hierarchy.[23] In a world where the concept of an independent nation-state was not present, foreign relations existed only as the dealings of one person with another. The rationale behind gift exchange in such a world was to reinforce this social hierarchy.

The key to the social relationship expressed in an exchange of *inw* is found in a unique statement in an inscription of a certain Amenhotep at Silsilah. In this passage he says, *wr.w ẖ3s.wt w3i [. . .] nḏt ḥm.f ẖr inw.sn nb:* "the princes of distant foreign lands [. . .] the *nḏt* of His Majesty bear all their *inw*." This partly broken passage demonstrates that those people who deliver *inw* are called *nḏt*. The *Wörterbuch* translates *nḏt* as "*Untertänen, Hörige,*" whereas Faulkner gives "serfs." Abd el-Mohsen Bakir Bakir believed that they were slaves, and David Lorton calls them "subjects."[24] Though Lorton does show by his examples that the *nḏt* position is defined by inferiority to the king, he does not recognize the connection with *inw*. A further passage also implies this connection. An inscription of the time of Thutmose III reads, *ii.n ḥm.f m 3w.t-ib ẖ3st tn tm.ti m nḏt.f . . . [. . .].w m sp wᶜ ẖr inw.sn*: "His Majesty returned joyfully, this foreign country gathered as his *nḏt* [. . .] at one time, bearing their *inw*."[25] The real meaning of the term *nḏt* when applied to foreigners is those people who are in a *inw*-exchanging relationship with the king. A *nḏt* is one who gives the king *inw*.

People became *nḏt* as a result of Amun's intervention. In a speech to Amenhotep, the god said, *di.i n.k rsyt m nḏt ḥm.k mḥty m ksw n b3w.k:* "I give to you the South as *nḏt* of Your Majesty, and the North bowing to your powers." The description of Northerners "bowing to your powers" parallels the usual description of how *inw* is delivered, thus further strengthening the link.[26] Turning foreigners into *nḏt,* therefore, is tantamount to saying that they will henceforth give him *inw.* Thus Thutmose I said, *iṯt.n.i st m nḫt ḫft wḏ.k irw grt m nḏt [. . .] srw ḫ3s.wt nb.wt m w3ḥ tp,* "I have seized them [other lands] in victory according to your command. Moreover, they were made *nḏt* [. . .], the magnates of every foreign land having bowed the head." This is a specific kind of claim where the king revealed that he had not destroyed an enemy, but rather that he had coerced him into the *inw*-exchanging relationship. The conquered have recognized his social superiority and henceforth will give him *inw.*

Being a *nḏt* also entailed receiving goods in return. Amenhotep son of Hapu recounted that he redistributed plunder (*ḥ3ḳ*) that the king had captured on the battlefield to the *nḏt.*[27] Thus the relationship was reciprocal. The king received *inw* from the *nḏt.* He in turn gave them commodities from the *ḥ3ḳ.*

The views of foreign princes on these exchanges of *inw* cannot be determined from the Egyptian sources. The Amarna Letters shed some light on this subject, however. The kings of Babylonia (EA 10:8; 11Rs.:19f; 9:19), Mittani (EA 19:34–42, 60), and Assyria (EA 16:19–21) all claimed that Egyptian kings had sent gold to their ancestors. Whether the Egyptians called this *inw* is not clear. Nevertheless, foreign kings felt free to request gold from Egypt.[28] Suppiluiuma also described in a letter to Akhenaton an exchange of gifts (*šulmana*) which he conducted with Amenhotep III (EA 41:17–20). These exchanges resulted in "good relations." Finally, Tushratta sent "gifts" to the king on the occasion of his marriage with Tatuhepa.[29] These gifts were called *tirḫata* (bride-price) in Akkadian (EA 27:14). Under similar conditions during the reign of Thutmose III, such bride-price gifts for the king were considered *inw* by the Egyptians.[30]

Such a bride-price is obviously a personal gift to the king, and thus *inw.*

The Uses of *Inw*

Goods that the Egyptians classified as *inw* were used by the king for his private expenses. This was not his only source of income, but because of the specific nature of gift-giving, gifts can usually only be used for specific purposes. There is evidence that the king used *inw* for food supplies in the inner palace as he did in the Middle Kingdom, for gifts to temples, and for rations for necropolis workmen.

Inw *Used at the Palace*

The hieratic jar dockets recovered from the palace of Amenhotep III at Malkata by William C. Hayes and later by David O'Connor provide an excellent idea of the foodstuffs consumed at the royal residence.[31] Even more revealing was the information recorded on the dockets concerning the sources of the materials. Though most of the foods bear no designation and were thus probably *ʿḳw, inw* is otherwise the most prominent designation given. Several commodities entered the palace under the rubric *inw.* These included wine, other drinks, curds, fat, fowl, and oil. The presence of these commodities marked *inw* points to a situation similar to that seen at the palace in P. Boulaq 18 during the Middle Kingdom. *Inw* formed a small but necessary portion of the goods consumed by the royal family. These goods were not considered to be part of the ordinary rations they received.

Inw *is Donated to Temples*

A second royal responsibility met with *inw* was donations to temples. Several statements show that *inw* was sometimes donated to the gods by the king.

14. *m33 Nḥsy.w rdy m tpy.w sḳr.w ʿnḫ r ḥtp-nṯr n Imn ḫft sḫrt kš ẖs.t ḥnʿ inw n ḫ3s.wt nb.wt rdi.n ḥm.f r ḥwt-nṯr Imn m ḥtr r tnw rnpt . . . in Inni*

Seeing the Nubians who were given as living prisoners to (be) the offerings of Amun after the overthrow of wretched Kush together with the *inw* of every foreign country which His Majesty gave to the Temple of Amun as a yearly levy . . . by Ineni.

Thutmose I–Hatshepsut[32]

Context: Caption in tomb of Ineni, Th.T. 81.

15. *mʿbʿ inw n ḫ3s.wt nb.wt inn.w m . . .*

"Offering *inw* of every foreign country which was brought from . . . "

Thutmose III[33]

Context: A caption to a relief showing the king offering to Amun. Karnak Temple.

16. *inw ʿ3 nn ḏr.f*

Great *inw* without limit.

Thutmose III[34]

Context: A list of offerings including animals and vessels.

17. *ʿš3 ḫt st šsp b3kt.t ḫ3s.wt nb.wt ms inw ʿš3.w m-b3ḥ it.i*

(It is) numerous of possessions, a place that receives the revenues of every land and great amounts of *inw* being offered before my father (Amun).

Amenhotep III[35]

Context: Description of a garden-house for Amun.

18. *[mʿbʿ] inw in ḥm.f n it.f Imn ḫft iw.f ḥr ḫ3st Rtnw ẖsy*

[Offering] *inw* by His Majesty to his father Amun after he returned from the foreign country of wretched Retenu.

Sety I[36]

Context: War scenes, Karnak Temple.

19. *ms inw m ḫ3st mḥty ii r tkk [t3š n] ḥm.f sm3 ᶜ.n ḥm.f . . . r mḥ šnᶜ n it.f Imn*

Presenting *inw* from the Northern foreign country that came to violate the [border of] His Majesty which His Majesty presented in order to fulfill the labor of his father Amun.

Ramesses II[37]

Context: Battle of Kadish reliefs, temple inscription.

20. *dhn.i n.f t3 mri ẖr inw.sn*

I signed over to him (Amun) Egypt, bearing their *inw.*

Ramesses III[38]

Context: List of donations to temples.

21. *nbw ḥḏ-nbw . . . i-di nsw Wsr-m3ᶜt-rᶜ mri Imn ᶜ.w.s p3 nṯr ᶜ3 m inw n nb ᶜ.w.s. r sḏf3 pr it.i špsy Imn-rᶜ*

Gold, electrum . . . which King Usermaatre-mery-Amun l.p.h. the great god, gave from the *inw* of the Lord, in order to provision the House of my noble father, Amun-Re.

Ramesses III[39]

Context: List of donations to temples.

22. *f3i.kwi im.s r ḫft-ḥr.k it.i Rᶜ ẖ3nn.kwi m nbw ḥḏ-nbw mi ḥfnw mst m inw m-b3ḥ.k m n3y.sn dpww di.w r pr-ḥḏ.k špsy m pr Itm*

I weighed in it (a scale) before you, Father Re. I inclined with great quantities of gold and electrum, offering from the *inw* before you from their coffers which are given to your noble treasury in the House of Atun.

Ramesses III[40]

Context: List of donations to temples.

23. *ms.i n.k inw ḳn m ᶜntyw*

May I offer to you very much *inw* consisting of myrrh.

Ramesses III[41]

Context: List of donations to temples.

Clearly, *inw* was at least one source from which the king met his responsibilities to the gods. This is not to say that other sources were not used as well for this purpose. This sort of exchange also fits the definition of exchange between unequal partners.

The King Pays Workers with Inw

Finally, there is evidence that the king could use *inw* to pay the necropolis workmen. In P. Turin 1903 a list of wages received for the necropolis workers is said to be "from the *inw* of Kush."[42]

Taken together with the evidence for the collection of *inw,* the disbursement methods of *inw* indicate strongly that it was a fund of commodities kept separate from other goods because they were subject to a special royal prerogative. The sources show a continued consciousness of goods' being *inw,* and therefore in a special category. These goods were subject to rules that differed from those applied to goods that were the king's in a strictly theoretical sense. This demonstrates again that *inw* was not part of the general redistributive economy in Egypt, but rather a special category of gift.

The Administration of *Inw* in the New Kingdom

The administration of the commodities called *inw* can best be analyzed in the New Kingdom by examining the specific operations or tasks mentioned in the texts and in captions accompanying relief scenes in tombs and temples. The following verbs are used with the word *inw* to indicate a particular operation: *ms,* "to present," *šsp,* "to receive," *m3,* "to view," *ẖbt,* "to withdraw," and *ẖrp,* "to administer."

Ms Inw

24. *ms inw ḫ3st rsy m nbw 3bw hbny iry-pᶜt ḥ3ty-ᶜ . . . s3-nsw imy-r pr ḫ3swt rsy nḥy*

Presenting the *inw* of the Southern foreign country consisting of gold, ivory, and ebony. . . . The Hereditary Noble, Mayor, King's Son and Overseer of the Southern Land, Nehi.

Thutmose III[43]

Context: Inscription of Nehi at Ellesiya near Ibrim.

25. *ms inw n Rtnw ḫrp.wt ḫ3s.wt mḥty.w ḥḏ-nbw ḫsbd mꜥfk3t ꜥ3.wt nb.wt nt [t3]-nṯr in wr.w n.w ḫ3s.wt nb.wt ii.sn r sn[mḥ] n nṯr nfr r dbḥ ṯ3w r fnd.sn in sš nswt m3ꜥ mrw.f imy-r mšꜥ sš nfrw Ṯ3nni*

Presenting the *inw* of Retenu and the taxes of the Northern foreign lands—electrum, lapis lazuli, turquoise, all costly stones of god's-land—by the chiefs of all foreign lands when they come to the Good God in order to request the breath of life for their noses—by the true royal scribe whom he loves, the Officer and Scribe of Recruits, Tjanni.

Thutmose III to Thutmose IV[44]

Context: Presentation scene in Th.T. 74.

26. *ms inw nb nfr n t3 mḥy m iw3w wnḏw 3ḫtyw 3pd.w rmw sšn nhtb ḫt nbt nfrt wꜥbt . . . in sš-nsw imy-r rwyt I3mw-nḏḥ m3ꜥ-ḫrw*

Presenting all the good *inw* of Lower Egypt consisting of long-horned cattle, short-horned cattle, *3ḫtyw*-cattle, fowl, fish, lotus buds, and every good pure thing . . . by the Royal Scribe and Overseer of the Portal, Yamunedjeh, justified.

Thutmose III[45]

Context: Caption to presentation scene in Theban Tomb 84.

27. *ist ḥm.f [. . .] ḫꜥw ḥr ispt nt ms inw ms [in]w rsy mḥty is iry-pꜥt Ḥr-m-ḥb m3ꜥ-ḫrw ꜥḥꜥ r gs i[spt] . . .*

Now His majesty appeared upon the throne of presenting *inw* that the *inw* of the South and the North might be presented. "Now it was at the side of the throne that the hereditary noble Horemheb stood."

Tutankhamun[46]
Context: The so-called Zizinia Block from the Memphite tomb of Horemheb.

28. *sḫ3 n.k p3 hrw n mst p3 inw iw.k msn m-b3ḥ [nsw] ẖr p3 sšd sr m itry m-b3ḥ ḥm.f ᶜ.w.s. wrw mšyt nw ḫ3st nb iw ᶜḥᶜ grg ḥr m33 p3 inw*
Remember the Day of Presenting the *inw* when you pass into the Presence beneath the Window, the nobles in two rows in the presence of His Majesty, l.p.h., the chiefs and envoys of every foreign land standing silent at viewing the *inw.*
Ramesside Period[47]
Context: Letter concerning Nubian revenues.

From the foregoing examples, the phrase *ms inw* seems to refer to a formal ceremony. The king was usually present while a high official presented the *inw* to him in the form of a parade. Most of these examples come from tomb scenes discussed by Cyril Aldred and Donald B. Redford. Though neither Aldred nor Redford was specifically concerned with the meaning of *inw* in their discussions, their observations on these scenes must be considered here.

Aldred remarked that others have viewed these tomb scenes as victory parades after battles.[48] He, however, preferred to interpret the scenes as "a public ceremony, following closely on the coronation rites in which the widespread sovereignty of the new ruler was recognized by his reception of gifts and homage from foreign nations as well as the representative of his own people."[49] Aldred's main objection to understanding these scenes as "victory parades" was that native Egyptians were often depicted presenting gifts along with the foreigners. Aldred further offered textual evidence from P. Turin 1882rt 1,2 which described giving "gifts of homage" to the king by Egyptians and foreigners after his coronation.[50] The word used for gift, however, is *brk,* a Semitic loan word, not the traditional Egyptian word *inw* found in these scenes when there is a caption. Thus it seems unlikely that the evidence of this papyrus can link these scenes to the coronation gifts described in the papyrus.

Redford has further commented that Aldred's other evidence, the use of the verb *ḫꜥi,* cannot be limited to coronations.[51] Moreover, the "tribute" scene in the Tomb of Huy can be shown not to have taken place early in Tutankhamun's reign. The same can be shown for the scenes of the tombs of Menkheperre-sonb and Rekhmire in the reign of Thutmose III. Redford persuasively argued that these scenes cannot be interpreted as part of the coronation, but rather that they depicted either a victory parade when shown in association with battle scenes or representations of the collection of annual imposts in which the tomb owner played a role.

In this connection, it is important to note the details of presenting the *inw* found in P. Koller. In line 4:7, the writer strongly implied that *inw* collection was an annual event. Moreover, by saying, "increase your contribution each year," he implied an element of voluntarism. One particular day seems to have been set aside for this event, which was called the "day of presenting *inw.*" (5:1) Furthermore, P. Koller informs us that on this day the nobles as well as chiefs and envoys of foreign countries were present before the king (5:2–3). This explains why the event was worthy of being recorded in a tomb. The deceased was claiming that he was among the nobles who had the honor of being in the presence of His Majesty during this ceremony. This evidence is also vital to an understanding of the phrase *m3 inw,* discussed below.

M3(3) Inw

29. *m3 inw nw t3 mḥw*
    Viewing the *inw* of the Delta.
    Thutmose III[52]
    Context: Caption from Tomb of Nebamun, Theban Tomb 24 in a food production scene.[53]

30. *m3 inw nw t3 mḥw m inw m ẖt nbt nn ḏr ᶜ.sn in [wḥm-nsw tp I3mw-nḏh] m3ᶜ-ẖrw*

Viewing the *inw* of the Delta consisting of *inw* and everything without limit by [the chief royal herald, Yamunedjeh] justified.

Thutmose III[54]

Context: Tomb of Yamunedjeh, North wall of inner chamber, food production scene.[55]

31. *m33 inw n pr-ḥḏ in imy-r3 k3t ẖrd n k3p P3- ḥḳ3-mn m3ᶜ-ẖrw*

Viewing the *inw* of the treasury by the Overseer of Works and Child of the Harim, Pahekamen, justified.

Dyn. 18[56]

Context: Deceased observes delivery, weighing, and recording of gold rings.

32. *ntf m3 inw n t3*

You are the one who views the *inw* of the land.

Thutmose III[57]

Context: Tomb of Rekhmire, *The Duties of the Vizier.*

The phrase *m3(3) inw* denoted at least three distinct activities during the New Kingdom. These activities spanned private food production, an official duty, and participation in the official ceremony of presenting *inw* to the king which has already been discussed.

Two tombs from the time of Thutmose III reveal the persistence of the Middle Kingdom view of *inw* as an element of food production even during this reign. Both Nebamun and Yamunedjeh included in their tombs scenes of *inw* of the Delta marsh presented to them. In Nebamun's tomb, this label is found in the fourth register of a four-register scene. The scene includes the deceased and his family fowling and fishing, a banquet, and a procession of Delta produce and vintage conveyed to him and his wife.[58] In the inner passage of Yamunedjeh's tomb, he was depicted viewing *inw* delivered to him and his wife from the Delta marshes by his brother. He received wine, figs, a bouquet, birds, and covered baskets of goods.[59] These two scenes are clearly dependent on the tradition first seen in the tomb of Baqet I of Beni Hasan. Like that tomb and those of Baqet's successors, *inw* was perceived as part of the commodities used to meet the deceased's food requirements. In both tombs family members delivered these goods to the deceased: a son in Nebamun's tomb, a brother in Yamunedjeh's tomb. There is no acknowledgment or perhaps even no belief that these offerings came to the deceased specifically as royal gifts. In fact, in Nebamun's tomb, the register of Delta *inw* was grouped with the fishing and fowling scene. The scene in Yamunedjeh's tomb is flanked by a fishing and fowling scene and a hunting scene. This implies that these two men who lived and worked in Thebes had access to Delta products on a regular basis in their tombs. This long-distance delivery could only have been effected through royal gifts. Most likely it was once again a reference to the royal redistribution of *inw* through a fishing/fowling ceremony in which these men participated (see chapter 3).

The scene in the tomb of Benya-Pahekamen depicts the deceased before three registers of men delivering, weighing, and recording gold rings. This is a second activity described as *m3 inw*. Here the deceased bore the title of "Overseer of Works." Most likely Benya was here performing a duty associated with this title, probably in association with the gilding of architectural elements.

The quotation from the *Duties of the Vizier* is also clearly a function of an office. This related to the vizier's responsibilities for overseeing the king's finances.

Šsp Inw

33. *šsp inw n wr n Pwnt in wpwyt-nsw*
    Receiving the *inw* of the Chief of Punt by the Royal Messenger.
    Hatshepsut[60]

Context: Caption in the Punt reliefs in the Mortuary Temple of Hatshepsut.

34. *šsp inw n Kš*
Receiving the *inw* of Kush.
Hatshepsut[61]
Context: Caption in the tomb of Senenmut.

35. *šsp inw n Hnw Stt n W3wt-Ḥr ḥnᶜ inw n ḫ3st rsy mḥtt*
Receiving the *inw* of Henou, Asia, the Ways of Horus, together with the *inw* of the Southern and Northern foreign countries.
Thutmose III[62]
Context: Caption to a presentation scene in the tomb of Puyemre.

36. *šsp inw [n] nḫt [ḥm.f]*
Receiving the *inw* [of] victory of [His Majesty].
Thutmose III[63]
Context: Caption to a presentation scene in the Tomb of Menkheperre-sonb.

37. *šsp inw innw n b3.w ḥm.f m ḥtr nt (?) rnpt m ᶜ wrw rtnw sḫnty m dpt r t3 mri [in] imy-r ᶜw n ḫ3st mḥtt sš-nsw ḏḥwty m3ᶜ-ḫrw*
Receiving the *inw* that was brought to the powers of His Majesty consisting of annual revenues by the Chiefs of Retenu and that was caused to go up stream by boat to Egypt by the Overseer of the Door of the Northern Foreign Country and Royal Scribe, Djeheuty.
Thutmose III[64]
Context: Inscription on a statue of Djeheuty.

38. *šsp inw n ḫ3st rsyt mᶜb3 inw n Pwnt inw n Rtnw inw n Kftyw mᶜb3 ḥ3ḳt n ḫ3s.wt nb.wt innw (n) b3.w ḥm.f nsw-bity Mn-Ḫpr-Rᶜ ᶜnḫ ḏt in . . . [Rḫ-mi-Rᶜ]*
Receiving the *inw* of the Southern foreign country. Offer-

ing the *inw* of Punt, the *inw* of Retenu, the *inw* of Keftiu and offering the plunder of all foreign countries which was brought to the powers of His Majesty, the King of Upper and Lower Egypt, Menkheperre, living forever, by . . . [Rekhmire].

Thutmose III[65]

Context: Caption in the tomb of Rekhmire.

39. Coming in peace of the Chiefs of Punt with bowing and inclined head bearing their *inw . . . in iry-pᶜt ḥ3ty-ᶜ mḥ-ib n nsw ḫnty t3.wy imy-r3 niwt ṯ3ty Rḫ-mi-Rᶜ šsp inw nb n ḫ3s.wt nb.wt innw n [b3.w] ḥm.f m nḫt[.f]* It was the hereditary prince and noble, the one who fills the King's heart, foremost of the Two lands, Mayor of the City, and Vizier Rekhmire who received all the *inw* of all foreign countries which was brought to the [powers] of His Majesty in [his] strength.

Thutmose III[66]

Context: Caption from the tomb of Rekhmire.

40. *šsp inw ḫ3st rsy mᶜb3 inw nw t3 mḥw m-b3ḥ imy-r niwt ṯ3ty Rḫ-mi-rᶜ*

Receiving the *inw* of the Southern foreign country and offering of *inw* of the Delta before the Mayor of the City and Vizier, Rekhmire.[67]

Context: Caption over a scribe who is writing, Tomb of Rekhmire.

41. *iw wḏ.n nb.i ṯsw b3k im r smr tp n ᶜḥ dhn.n.f sw r imy-r3 k3.w ḥm-nṯr tp n wrt ḥk3 wḥm.n.f rdit.f r imy-r niwt wpt-m3ᶜt diw m-ḥr.f r šsp inw ḫ3st rsyt mḥtt r pr-ḥḏ n nsw*

My lord commanded that this servant might be raised to First Friend of the Palace, he having appointed him as Overseer of Cattle, and First Prophet of Hike. He continued [by] appointing him as Mayor of the City and . . . ? . . . giving him responsibility for receiving the *inw* of the Northern and Southern foreign countries for the royal treasury.

Ramesses II[68]

Context: Tomb biography of Paser.

The term *šsp inw* was used to refer to at least three different administrative acts. It was used at the initial reception of the *inw* from the donor, the assuming of responsibility for the *inw* after the official presentation to the king, and the storing of the *inw* until it was needed for other purposes.

Examples 33 and 37 clearly demonstrate that a royal representative officially accepted the *inw* from a local chief on behalf of the king. In a case where the *inw* was occasional in nature, as in Punt, this task was handled by a *wpwty-nsw* as leader of the expedition. In West Asia, where *inw* was collected annually during the reign of Thutmose III, it appears that at least some goods were collected in Byblos for forwarding by ship to Egypt. This task was carried out by the Overseer of the Door of the Northern Foreign Country.

On arrival in Egypt, the *inw* was formally presented to the king in the *ms inw* ceremony. After this ceremony the *inw* became the responsibility of the vizier (exx. 34, 35, 36, 38, 39). Rekhmire, for example, claimed that a report of all *inw* was made directly to him.[69] The vizier's office must then have divided up the commodities according to type and had them sent to the proper storage area. Example 41 shows that this area was the royal treasury. Here once again the term was used for the scribe who worked in the treasury. The list the scribe is preparing of the *inw* might well be called a "receipt."

In conclusion, the term *šsp inw* implied an assumption of responsibility for the goods as part of a chain of bureaucracy that guides the *inw* from the hands of the donor/chief to Egypt, and from the official presentation ceremony to storage. Though details are lacking in the preserved record, it is clear that there was a well-defined processing procedure for the *inw* from the donor to the royal treasury.

ẖb Inw

42. *ntf ir ẖbt inw n gsw-prw*
"He (the vizier) is the one who withdraws *inw* from the storage."
Thutmose III[70]
Context: *The Duties of the Vizier*, Tomb of Rekhmire.

The word *ẖb* has the basic meaning of "reduce, subtract."[71] The root is also known in Demotic and Coptic with a similar semantic range. The *Wörterbuch* III, 252, however, lists the expression *ẖb inw* separately with the meaning "*Gaben sammeln; Abgaben einziehen.*" The *Wörterbuch* notes that in the Greek Period *inw* was often followed by the genitive and the donor or an "*m*" with the name of a country, meaning "from."

On the basis of P. Harageh 3114, Paul C. Smithers argued that the word *ẖb* retained its basic meaning "reduce" in this expression and construed it as "extraction of dues."[72] He cited one Ptolemaic example from Edfu which he read *it.k kmt ḥḳ3.k Dšsrt ẖb.k inw Iwntyw*, "May you seize the Black Land, Rule the Red Land, and extract the dues of the Nubians." Similar examples occur elsewhere in Edfu and at Dendera.[73]

If the word *ẖb* retained its basic meaning of reduce or subtract in the expression *ẖb inw*, it is difficult to follow Smithers's logic. Extraction of dues is not really related to the basic meaning. Though this meaning appears to make sense in his Ptolemaic example, it does not clarify the one New Kingdom example.

The *gs-pr* was a place where *inw* was stored. This is clear from the Biography of Duaherneheh where he describes his duties as Overseer of the *gs-pr*.[74] Here we are told that he controlled "great amounts of *inw*." The meaning of *ẖbt inw n gs-pr* would then more likely mean to reduce the amount of *inw* stored there. This should be thought of as "withdrawing *inw*" for use. This situation would explain a subtraction or diminishing of the *inw*.

If this theory is accepted, however, it does not clarify the Ptolemaic example quoted by Smithers. This can be explained by the confusion Černý noted in the Late Period between the roots *ḫb* and *ḫb3*.[75] The word *ḫb3* means "to hack up,"[76] which would be more parallel to the other phrases used in the Edfu inscription. The sequence then would be, "May you seize the Black Land, Rule the Red Land, and hack up the *inw* of the Nubians." Because the word used for Nubians is *Iwntyw,* we might expect the inclusion of the word *inw* as a word play with *Iwntyw,* combined with a larger play on the expression *ḫb inw.*

Storage Facilities and Tasks Completed There

43. *iw ḫrp.n.i iw3 wn-ḏw ht-ʿ3 šd nn ḏrw.f inw ʿš3 m-tp ḥr [sic] tp*
I controlled the long-horned cattle and the short-horned cattle, the *ht-ʿ3*-geese and the *šd*-geese without limit and great amounts of the best *inw.*
Hatshepsut[77]
Context: Tomb biography of Duaherneheh.

44. . . . *inw.sn ḥr psḏ.sn r mḥ rwyt*
. . . their *inw* on their backs in order to fill the gate.
Thutmose III[78]
Context: Tomb of Ineni.

45. *[ip] inw n W3.wt-Ḥr ip inw n ḫ3s.wt*
[Counting] the *inw* of the Ways of Horus, counting the *inw* of the foreign countries.
Thutmose III[79]
Context: Caption to presentation scene in the tomb of Puyemre.

The general administration of the *inw,* once it reached storage, was under the Overseer of the *gs-pr,* though it could also be stored in the gate. Once the *inw* was inside the storage, inventories were made. Within the storehouse, the *inw* seems to be organized according to its identity as *inw* rather than according to kind of commodity.

Conclusions about *Inw* in the New Kingdom

The New Kingdom sources add much to the description of *inw*. They show that it was neither trade nor tribute but rather represented an official gift exchanged between the king and a variety of other people, both Egyptian and foreign. The foreigners were treated in the same manner in this system with no regard to their degree of dependence on Egypt or on the establishment of Egyptian hegemony in their native country. The *inw*-exchanging relationship merely demonstrated the Egyptian king's superiority to other men in the social hierarchy. The system was sanctioned by the gods and provided the king with additional revenue. A large bureaucracy was maintained to account for the *inw* from the time it left foreign soil to the formal presentation ceremony, during periods of storage, and finally its use to reward men for royal service or to pay an obligation to the gods, or as raw material in royal building projects.

Inw bore only an indirect relationship to Egyptian establishment of hegemony outside its traditional borders. An exchange of *inw* between the king and another prince was an expression of each ruler's place in the social hierarchy of Near Eastern potentates. The exchange of *inw* with more and more distant foreigners was clearly a direct result of the king's wider influence and hegemony. He increased his social status by his conquests. This enhanced status and prestige was recognized by the exchange of *inw*, but this exchange was not an acknowledgment of hegemony over a particular area. When a king recounted that foreign princes sent *inw* to him, he was claiming that his increased status was recognized throughout the world. He was not asserting that he ruled an area when he said that he received *inw* from its prince. The monumental sources from the New Kingdom thus provide a view of the meaning of *inw* with regard to foreign relations.

Chapter Five

Conclusions:

Evidence, Bias, Models

This study of *inw* has been based on 179 textual uses of the term ranging in date from Dynasty 0 through Dynasty 20, a period exceeding two thousand years. The evidence was drawn from six categories of textual sources that are not uniformly preserved in the different periods of Egyptian history. The categories include jar labels or seals in archaeological context, royal inscriptions written for public consumption, royal governmental documents on papyrus not intended for the public, privately commissioned inscriptions and captions to scenes written by those dependent on or subject to royal power, literary texts (mostly written from a royal point of view), and provincial inscriptions of independent local rulers.

Preservation of each kind of evidence is wildly uneven. Jar labels and seals are known only from the Archaic Period (Dynasties 1–3) and one reign of Dynasty 18. Royal inscriptions for public consumption are not extant from Dynasties 1 to 3 and are extremely rare in the Old and Middle Kingdoms. Royal government records now available to scholars comprise an infinitesimal percentage of what must have existed at all periods of Egyptian history. Georges Posener has calculated that every temple produced 120 meters of papyrus records per year.[1] Yet the only archives available for this study come from one Old Kingdom mortuary establishment, one Middle Kingdom mortuary establishment, and a brief period at the palace of Sobekhotep II of Dynasty 13. No New Kingdom text of this sort is known. Privately composed inscriptions belonging to those under royal authority are perhaps best represented across a broad time spectrum, with eight from the Old Kingdom, fifteen from the Middle Kingdom, and twenty in the New Kingdom. Finally, inscriptions of independent nomarchs are only represented in the First Intermediate Period and early Middle Kingdom. This class of document presumably only existed in this period.

Most of the texts quoted here were written to promote a particular bias. Royal inscriptions, private tomb inscriptions from Memphis, Thebes, and Aswan, and many literary texts were written to promote the interests of the central government. They all represented the royal point of view. The royal government documents accept the royal bias without the same degree of tendentiousness. They were in no way concerned with promoting a particular view of what *inw* was; rather, their writers assumed that *inw* would arrive from certain sources and be redistributed for particular ends. These documents therefore are the closest to raw fact without an overlay of opinion that scholars possess. The same could be said of jar labels and seals found in archaeological context. They exist as evidence for modern scholars and need not be questioned as propaganda, though certainly they must be interpreted to acquire any sort of meaning, and any interpretation is open to modern debate. Inscriptions written by independent provincial rulers represent a bias against central government. To that extent, the existence of these documents creates a much more complex picture of the Egyptian view of *inw*. These documents serve to remind modern scholars that there was more than one Egyptian view of a cultural process. With the added variable of two thousand years of change and development, the modern interpreter must be modest in claiming completeness or access to truth in a description of *inw*, its exchange, and its meaning for the Egyptians.

Nevertheless, certain statements about *inw* can be made with confidence. First, *inw* was always part of a redistributive process. Second, in periods of central control, the king was always a party to an economic transaction described as *inw*. Third, in most periods both parties to the transaction were human individuals of unequal status, though independent nomarchs of the First Intermediate Period and early Middle Kingdom created a new source of *inw* by interpreting the produce of the marsh as their own *inw* from nature. The regular exchange of *inw* between individuals of unequal status from both higher to lower, and lower to higher allows a modern translation for the word of "official gift."

These "official gifts" comprised a basic component of ancient Egyptian society in the earliest period. It has already been suggested that official gift-giving was a custom that began before Dynasty 1 and was continued into the Archaic Period by the kings of a newly unified Egypt. The textual evidence of royal and noble tombs in this period, when considered in its proper archaeological context, is unequivocal. A comparatively more complex bureaucracy in the Old Kingdom used official gift exchange differently from the kings of the Archaic Period. The earlier kings were likely less removed from their followers than were the kings of the Old Kingdom.

The Old Kingdom does provide unbiased evidence in the form of the Abu Sir papyri. In a more complex setting, official gifts have been transformed into part of the income and disbursements of a busy institution. The elements of gift exchange are still present because the deceased king was one of the partners to the transaction. Egyptian culture's conservatism allowed it to preserve an already ancient cultural custom and use it for contemporary purposes.

The official gifts conveyed to the tombs of Sekhemkare and Ptahhotep II are more similar to the Archaic Period tradition. In these Old Kingdom tombs of nobles, personified royal estates were depicted conveying essential foods for the use of the deceased. Perhaps in their unplundered state, jars labeled in a manner similar to those found in the earlier periods were included in these tombs. In this case the reliefs on the walls attest to a redundant system that assured food offerings and incidentally preserved this information about redistribution to modern scholars.

The evidence for redistribution in the Middle Kingdom is clear for the period after the central government was firmly restored. The biography of Khnumhotep II emphasized the importance that loyal officials of the central government attached to the rewards of the king's gift. Yet the gifts are meant for the support of the tomb as they were in the Archaic Period and Old Kingdom. This was perhaps a result of the new views of *inw* developed by independent nomarchs of Dynasty 11 and early Dynasty 12.

The Old Kingdom institutional use of *inw* was paralleled at the mortuary installation at Illahun. Here official gifts were passed from town to temple, from palace to temple, and from temple to others reflecting a microcosm of the complexity of Egyptian society in the Middle Kingdom. P. Boulaq 18 also reveals the importance of gifts for support of the palace routine in life. The king distributed these gifts both to the Inner and Outer Palace, using them to meet various shortfalls or unexpected expenses.

Redistribution of official gifts in the New Kingdom is attested at the palace, as gifts to temples, and as a source of rations for workmen. There are no records from mortuary installations that could provide a parallel to the Abu Sir and Illahun papyri. The Turin papyrus, which indicates that *inw* was used to support workers at Deir el Medinah, suggests that the same practice was known in the New Kingdom as was found earlier.

The king's role in this official gift exchange was fundamental from the very beginning. Every jar label of a gift exchange in Dynasties 1 and 2 specifically mentions the king. This fact is to some extent responsible for the confusion in the literature over the ownership of the Saqqara tombs of the Archaic Period. The large number of royal gifts at Saqqara is one factor that misled Walter Emery into thinking that these tombs were cenotaphs of the king. The second type of evidence emphasizing the importance of royal involvement comes from New Kingdom exchanges with foreign potentates. The evidence here is also very explicit, always stressing that foreign chiefs dealt directly with the king when giving official gifts. The presence of this evidence at both the beginning and end of the period being studied adds weight to the speculation that it must also have been true in Dynasties 11 and 12 in areas under royal control. The absence of direct evidence of this kind of intense royal involvement in gift exchange probably creates a false picture of the view of the kings of Dynasty 12. It is here that the model of a *inw* exchange allows speculation with some degree of confidence and that the model is most useful.

The complexity obscured by the model is, however, restored, through the evidence preserved from Middle Egypt in Dynasties 11 and 12. Here a minority ancient Egyptian view of *inw* as gifts of nature to the nomarch can be discerned. At Beni Hasan by the time of Baqet I, gifts came to the local ruler both from people and from nature. This interpretation of *inw* seemingly was not present in the previous period. Its development was likely limited to Middle Egypt. It continued until the local nomarchs fully acknowledged the central authority. This development had a lasting effect on the way these official gifts were depicted subsequently. In the Archaic Period and through the Old Kingdom, the nobleman's tomb itself was supported through official gifts. Nomarchs also used official gifts as a means of support for their tombs. Once the central authority was restored, however, these gifts were no longer as important to the support of nomarch's tombs. Tomb biography stressed their use in life, but not as much in death. Furthermore, the depiction of official gifts found in New Kingdom Theban tombs was quite different from the tombs of the earlier periods. In the New Kingdom, nobles depict official gifts made to the king in life by foreign princes. They do this to promote their own status by proclaiming their presence at the ceremony. Tomb owners also receive gifts themselves for support of their tombs from nature, a practice borrowed from the Middle Kingdom. Here is development along a second track that the original model of *inw* could not have predicted: a secondary kind of gift from nature to the tomb owner, which is found in tombs of early Dynasty 18. Though the original Archaic Period meaning of *inw* was clearly continued by kings of Dynasties 18 and 19, it existed alongside *inw* from nature for nobles, at least in the earliest part of Dynasty 18. Though it would be simpler to assume that this second track was acknowledged at the royal center through a festival of the Fisher/Fowler of the Two Ladies, the true meaning of the festival cannot be determined with the present evidence beyond the Middle Kingdom.

Festivals including official gift exchange among people and from nature to a ruler were different in kind. Festivals of official gift presentation and redistribution between people are known from tomb representations and descriptions on papyrus. The Old Kingdom preserves only a festival of redistribution to nobles, whereas provincial tombs of Dynasties 11 and 12 depicted both collection of *inw* by the nomarch in the earlier period and redistribution from the king to the local prince in the later period. A New Kingdom festival for the presentation of official gifts to the king was depicted in Amarna and described in a papyrus of the Ramesside Age. Once again, the uneven preservation of evidence allows only the broadest outline of these festivals to be constructed.

The festivals in which *inw* exchanges were made seem to include at least two elements: a parade of offering bearers observed by the deceased and wrestling matches. The tomb owner conveyed different intentions in different periods when he depicted himself attending such parades. Ptahhotep II emphasized the support his tomb endowment received from the king. This is clear because the donors here were royally owned estates. When Merire II and other New Kingdom officials represented parades of foreigners and Egyptians delivering official gifts to the king, they stressed their status by showing that they were among the nobles who attended this ceremony in the king's presence.

The redistribution ceremony depicted in the Old Kingdom is the Thoth Festival. The festival calendar from the time of

Neuserre places it on I Akhet 20.[2] It is therefore part of the festivals that began the year.

The presence of wrestlers in the scene of *inw* redistribution to Ptahhotep II and *inw* collection in the tombs of Baqet I and II and Ukhhotep I of Meir raise the question of whether the Egyptians celebrated memorial games for the deceased that included *inw* redistribution.

Decker has demonstrated that wrestling is depicted at many types of ceremonies in ancient Egypt.[3] It was depicted at the presentation of official gifts to the living king at Amarna and at other festivals where the king appeared. Wrestlers were also depicted beneath the "Window of Appearances" at Medinet Habu.[4] Most important for an understanding of the scenes of wrestling and official gift presentation, wrestling appears in the tomb of Amenmesse (Th.T. 19) from the time of Ramesses I and Sety I.[5] Here two wrestlers grapple within the mortuary temple of Thutmose III. Decker has suggested that these wrestlers were participating in a memorial ritual for the deceased king.[6] It is possible that the wrestlers in the tombs of Ptahhotep II and in the Middle Kingdom provincial tombs were also present at a memorial ceremony. Official gifts in this interpretation were delivered as part of this ritual. A second possibility would be that the scenes show funerary games, part of the burial ritual itself.[7] In either case, official gifts were placed here in a particular kind of context when redistributed to the nobles.

The "Day of Presenting Official Gifts" is best illustrated in the tomb of Merire II in Amarna.[8] A partially preserved caption to the scene along with a letter in P. Koller give a relatively full description of the events at the festival. At Amarna the festival occurred II Peret 8. It cannot be associated with other festivals and may have occurred on another date in other reigns. Both Akhenaton and Nefertity appeared on the throne while the chiefs of foreign countries presented their gifts. The relief shows the presence of the nobles in addition to foreign chiefs, but P. Koller stresses that they are there to observe the ceremony.

Earlier in Dynasty 18 officials only rarely depicted the king in their tombs.[9] Thutmose III appeared in Rekhmire's tomb only in the scene where the king appointed him vizier. This is the reason that the king is in close proximity to the scene of Rekhmire receiving foreign tribute. In the tombs of Puyemre (Th.T. 39), Ineni (Th.T. 81), and Antef (Th.T. 155), each owner depicted himself performing his own role in receiving official gifts for the king. Puyemre included the royal cartouche in the scene to clarify that the ultimate owner of the gifts is the king.[10] Because the scenes were so carefully focused in the earlier tombs, it has not always been clear that these scenes represent the same activity found in Merire II's tomb. Yet the basic ceremony must have been similar both in early Dynasty 18 and the Amarna Period. Only the means of illustrating it changed in the later period.

Gifts from nature might also have been presented to the nobles by the king in a ceremony or festival. This evidence is even less complete than the evidence of the Thoth Festival and the "Day of Presenting Official Gifts." It included many elements that remain obscure. When celebrated in times of strong central government, the king appeared as "Fisher/Fowler of the Two Ladies" (*Wḥ*ᶜ*-Nbty*). He redistributed the catch as official gifts after hunting birds and fishing. The text of the Annals of Amenemhet II is the only textual description of this ceremony and one of the very few attestations of this manifestation of the king. The king was replaced by Sekhet, the deified marsh, in Middle Kingdom provincial tombs before central government fully established its control. This type of scene continued into early Dynasty 18 as one means of receiving support for the nobleman's mortuary establishment. Yet the presentation of these products to the deceased by a relative suggests that these scenes were a reinterpretation of the Middle Kingdom custom. No date can be attached to this ceremony. It could be that in the tombs it represented a continuous process rather than the distinct event described in the time of Amenemhet II.

Once the official gifts reached the royal storehouses, they remained a distinct group of objects not counted with other provisions that the king acquired through taxation. In the Abu Sir Papyri, the Illahun Papyri and P. Boulaq 18 *inw* was used as an accounting term, heading rows of numbers. In general it formed a small percentage of the provisions used by the king, his family, and his other retainers. The official gift's importance remained its social dimension, its use as an expression of relationships rather than its economic value.

In addition to determining the place of the official gift in ancient Egyptian culture, this study has also tested an explicit model of economic transactions in ancient Egypt. The model to a great extent has structured the presentation of the evidence and has dominated its analysis. The model itself has been described and defended in chapter 1 and has proved its usefulness throughout these pages. A further word must be said about the value of models in general as an approach to writing the history of ancient Egypt.

All historians approach the evidence with a mental template that structures the evidence which they collect and evaluate. Trade, tribute, tax, and gift each correspond to an implicit concept in the author's mind of a modern means of exchanging goods. The greatest value of the model is to force a clear and explicit definition of that concept before applying it to Egypt. This statement of what the author actually means by using a particular word forces the realization that every act of translation or analysis implicitly compares an ancient word or concept with a modern one. This statement of assumptions can be a great help in avoiding the trap of removing a particular custom from the total cultural system. By the use of the model of the economy, the official gift can be viewed as part of a total system and not an exotic anomaly.

The second virtue of a model as a means of writing ancient history is the tools it provides for filling gaps in the evidence. In the study of ancient Egypt this is particularly useful. It has been stressed here that each period of Egyptian history provides different kinds of archaeological and textual evidence. These differences in evidence type artificially create apparent differences or developments from one period to the next. Historians must exercise constant judgment about the evidence that is missing as well as what is present. Perhaps the greatest gap in ancient Egyptian historical evidence is the lack of inscribed royal monuments with continuous historical texts from the Old and Middle Kingdoms of the sort that are so numerous for the New Kingdom. This deprives modern scholars of the king's own words and thoughts in even the very controlled and filtered form that exists for the Thutmoside and Ramesside kings. This gap also makes comparisons among the different periods impossible without the use of models. Again, the model helps define what is missing and clearly marks when assumption and intuition have taken over from evidence in the reconstruction of a historical development.

As valuable as the model is for making assumptions explicit, filling gaps in the evidence, and differentiating between assumption and evidence, there are very real pitfalls in its use. First, once a model is formulated, it is sometimes difficult to include the evidence that does not fit the preconceived plan. There is a temptation to minimize the value of dissenting evidence and thereby impose rigid uniformity on the Egyptians. This danger is of course present with or without model use, inasmuch as the bias of the textual sources is so pronounced. Thus it is particularly important to weigh the bias of a source and include the dissenting voices in the final synthesis. Though historians will never be able to recover the full complexity of competing opinions among the ancient Egyptians, they should not collaborate with the ancient royal propagandists to create a uniform and placid picture of ancient Egyptian thought.

Finally, care must be given not to regard a static model as true for the full length of Egyptian history. Over the course of two thousand years of Pharaonic history under consideration here, official gift exchange must have changed radically. These changes cannot be described from the existing evidence. It can be acknowledged that the fit between the model and the facts was more or less tight in different time periods. The degree of fit can be determined to the extent possible from existing evidence.

In sum, the model when used carefully promises to provide a tool for building a new, less ethnocentric vision of ancient Egypt that will be more modest in its claims but more trustworthy in its truths.

Appendix

Translations of Inw

The following is a small sampling of translations of the word *inw* as it has been defined in English, French, and German. Source information follows each translation. These translations attest to the difficulty of equating the Egyptian word with one European concept.

Abgaben: *Wb.* I, 93; W. Helck, *Wirtschaftsgeschichte* (1975), 24–25 nn.21, 24.

Allotment: W. Emery, *The Tomb of Hemaka* (1938), 35–39.

Apport: P. Lacau & J-Ph. Lauer, *Pyramide*, vol. 5 (1965), 111; D. Meeks, *Année*, passim; P. Posener-Kriéger, *Archives* (1976), 667.

Contributions: F. L. Griffith, "Account" (1891), 105–106; P. Davies, *Ptahhetep*, vol. 1 (1900), 11.

Dinge: L. Borchardt, "Rechnungsbuch" (1890), 76.

Diplomatic gifts: R. O. Faulkner, *CDME* (1962), 22.

Don: P. Lacau & J.-Ph. Lauer, *Pyramide*, vol. 5 (1965), 111.

Dues: F. L. Griffith, *Petrie* (1898), 43, 45, 63; R. O. Faulkner, *CDME* (1962), 22; P. Smithers, "Tax" (1941), 75.

Du: P. Posener-Kriéger, *Archives* (1976), 633n.1.

Einkunfte: L. Borchardt, "Rechnungsbuch" (1890), 70, 73, 76.

Einnahmen: L. Borchardt, "Rechnungsbuch" (1890), 77.

Geschenk: *Wb.* I, 93; H. Brunner, *Texte,* 17.

Gift: E. A. W. Budge, *Egyptian* (1920), 56; A. Gardiner, *AEO,* vol. 1 (1947), *127, *177.

Gifts from palace: R. O. Faulkner, *CDME* (1962), 22; J. Breasted, *ARE* (1906–1907), passim; W. Emery, *The Tomb of Hemaka,* (1938), 35–39; E. Edel, "Inschriften" (1955), 71–72; W. C. Hayes, "Notes" (1951), 158; M. Lichtheim, *AEL,* vol. 1 (1976), 23–27.

Goods: D. Lorton, *Juridical* (1974), 102.

Herbeigebrachten Gaben: *Wb.* I, 93.

Income: E. A. W. Budge, *Egyptian* (1920), 56.

Increase: E. A. W. Budge, *Egyptian* (1920), 56.

Lieferungen: *Wb.* I, 93.

Livraison: P. Posener-Kriéger, *Archives* (1976), 667.

Merchandises: P. Montet, *Reliques* (1937), 18.

Offerings: E. A. W. Budge, *Egyptian* (1920), 56; P. Newberry, *El Bersheh,* vol. 1 (1893–94), 38.

Owner of merchandise: E. A. W. Budge, *Egyptian* (1920), 56.

Presents: P. Newberry, *El Bersheh,* vol. 2 (1893–94), 41.

Produce: J. Breasted, *ARE* (1906–1907), passim; R. O. Faulkner, *CDME* (1962), 22; A. Gardiner, "Inscriptions" (1908), 124; A. Blackman, *Meir,* vol. 1 (1914), 28; P. Newberry, *Beni Hasan,* vol. 1 (1893), 34, 69; B. Kemp, "Imperialism" (1978), 14.

Produckte: *Wb.* I, 93.

Products: P. Newberry, *Beni Hasan,* vol. 1 (1893), 64; J. Breasted, *ARE* (1906—1907), passim; E. A. W. Budge, *Egyptian* (1920), 56; A. Blackman, *Meir,* vol. 1 (1914), 28.

Produits: P. Montet, *Reliques* (1937), 13–18.

Quarry of hunter: R. O. Faulkner, *CDME* (1962), 22.

Revenues: E. A. W. Budge, *Egyptian* (1920), 56; B. Kemp, "Imperialism" (1978), 14; M. A. Leahy, *Excavations,* vol. 4 (1978), 2, 6, 31, 33, 34, 35, 36, 37, 48n.11.

Something brought in: E. A. W. Budge, *Egyptian* (1920), 56.

Trade: C. Aldred, "Foreign" (1970), 111.

Tribut(s): D. Meeks, *Année* (1980), passim

Tribute: B. Gunn, "Inscriptions" (1923), 162; F. L. Griffith, *Petrie* (1898), 63; J. Breasted, *ARE* (1906–1907), passim; E. A. W. Budge, *Egyptian* (1920), 56; W. M. F. Petrie, *Royal,* vol. 2 (1893), 53; W. C. Hayes, "Inscriptions" (1951), 158; R. O. Faulkner, *CDME* (1962), 22; P. Newberry, *Beni Hasan,* vol. 1 (1893), 25; D. Lorton, "So-called" (1973), 66; H. Grapow, *Studien* (1947), 27–32; A. Spalinger, "Critical" (1977), 45, 53n.25; A. Schulman, "Diplomatic" (1979), 192; M. Liverani, "Memorandum" (1973), 193; B. Trigger, *Nubia* (1976), 22; B. Kemp, "Imperialism" (1978), 14.

Tributgaben: *Wb.,* vol. 1 93.

Wages: E. A. W. Budge, *Egyptian* (1920), 56.

Notes

Chapter One

1. A. Gordon, "The Context and Meaning of the Ancient Egyptian Word INW from the Proto-Dynastic Period to the End of the New Kingdom" (unpublished Ph.D. dissertation, University of California, Berkeley, 1983), 63; P. Kaplony, *Die Inschriften der ägyptischen Frühzeit,* vol. 1 (Wiesbaden, 1963), 14–15, vol. 2, 1114, vol. 3, pl. 45, no. 161.2.

2. For example, M. de Rochemonteix and E. Chassinat, *Le Temple d'Edfou,* vol. 1 (Paris, 1897), 188.

3. E. Bleiberg, "Aspects of the Political, Religious, and Economic Basis of Egyptian Imperialism during the New Kingdom" (unpublished Ph.D. dissertation, University of Toronto, 1984).

4. E. Bleiberg, "Commodity Exchange in the Annals of Thutmose III," *JSSEA* 11 (1981): 107–10.

5. For preliminary formulations of this hypothesis, see E. Bleiberg, "Commodity," 107–10; "The King's Privy Purse During the New Kingdom: An Examination of *INW,*" *JARCE* 21 (1984): 155–67; and "The Redistributive Economy in New Kingdom Egypt: An Examination of *B3KW(T),*" *JARCE* 25 (1988): 157–68. For a dissenting view, see R. Müller-Wollermann, "Bemerkungen zu den sogenan-

nten Tributen," *GM* 66 (1983): 81–94, and "Waren Austausch im Ägypten des Alten Reiches," *JESHO* 28 (1985): 135 ff.

6. N. Georgescu-Roegen, *Analytical Economics: Issues and Problems* (Cambridge, Mass., 1966), 362.

7. On the existence of a *suq* as opposed to a true market, see C. Eyre, "Work and Organization of Work in the Old Kingdom," in M. A. Powell, *Labor in the Ancient Near East* (New Haven, 1987), 5–47, esp. 31. On the origins of money in Greece, see P. Grierson, "The Origins of Money," *REC* 1 (1978): 1–36.

8. G. Dalton, ed., *Primitive and Modern Economics: Essays of Karl Polanyi* (Boston, 1971), xiv.

9. Ibid., xxxv.

10. K. Polanyi in G. Dalton, ed., *Primitive,* 9–10.

11. Ibid., 119.

12. Most important, J. J. Janssen, "Economic History during the New Kingdom," *SAK* 3 (1975): 131; R. Müller-Wollermann, "Waren," 135 ff.

13. The following discussion is greatly influenced by R. Halperin, "Polanyi, Marx, and the Institutional Paradigm in Economic Anthropology," *REC* 6 (1984): 245–72, and "The Concept of the Formal in Economic Anthropology," *REC* 7 (1985): 339–68.

14. R. Halperin, "Polanyi," 257.

15. M. Herskovits, *Economic Anthropology* (New York, 1952), vii, my emphasis.

16. R. Firth, *Themes in Economic Anthropology* (London, 1967), 4, my emphasis.

17. D. North, "Markets and Other Allocation Systems in History: The Challenge of Karl Polanyi," *JEEH* 6 (1977), 703–16, and "Government and the Cost of Exchange in History," *JEH* 44 (1984): 255–64. Though Polanyi, working with A. L. Oppenheim, developed his theories with Mesopotamia in mind, students of the Mesopotamian economy have become aware of new evidence that casts some doubt on its applicability for all aspects of the situation there. For example, see J. Renger, "Patterns of Non-Institutional Trade and Non-Commercial Exchange in Ancient Mesopotamia," in A. Archi, ed., *Circulation of Goods in Non-Palatial Context in the Ancient Near East* (Rome, 1984), 31–124.

18. D. North, "Government," 256.

19. D. North, "Challenge," 709.

20. Ibid., 712.

21. For example, see the advice given on achieving the best in

life through service to Amun in *P. Anastasi* IV, 3:3 ff. Translation in R. Caminos, *Late Egyptian Miscellanies* (Oxford, 1954), 137–38.

22. D. North, "Government," 264.

23. M. Silver, *Economic Structures of the Ancient Near East* (Totowa, N.J., 1985), 82–85, 135–36; B. Kemp, "The Birth of Economic Man," *Ancient Egypt: Anatomy of a Civilization* (London, 1989), 232–60.

24. See H. Fischer, "The Nubian Mercenaries of Gebelein during the First Intermediate Period," *Kush* 9 (1961): 44–80, esp. 46–48. Translation also available in M. Lichtheim, *Ancient Egyptian Literature,* vol. 1, (Berkeley, 1976) 90.

25. See H. Fischer, "Old Kingdom Inscriptions in the Yale Gallery," *MIO* 7 (1960): 299–315, esp. 308n.18.

26. H. Fischer, "Nubian," 49.

27. For example, in Memphis, see D. Jeffreys and J. Málek, "Memphis 1984," *JEA* 72 (1986): 5, and "Memphis 1986, 1987," *JEA* 74 (1988): 20. See also references in B. Kemp, *Birth*: in Amarna, 288–89, 296, 299; in forts, 173, 175, 177–78, 195; in Kahun 153–57; in the Ramesseum, 192, 196, 234–35; and in Thebes, 191, 192, 194, 253.

28. Conveniently in *AEL,* vol. 2, (Berkeley, 1976), 170.

29. For the text and commentary, see T. G. H. James, *The Hekanakhte Papers and Other Early Middle Kingdom Documents* (New York, 1962). For additional commentary on the economic situation represented there, see K. Baer, "The Low Price of Land in Ancient Egypt," *JARCE* 1 (1962): 25–45, and "An Eleventh Dynasty Farmer's Letters" *JAOS* 83 (1963): 1–19. The Twelfth Dynasty date is now generally accepted, see D. Arnold, "Amenemhet and the Early Twelfth Dynasty at Thebes," *MMJ* 26 (1991): 5–48, esp. 36–38; see also H. Goedicke, *Studies in the Hekanakhte Papers* (Baltimore, 1984), 8–10.

30. K. Baer, "Eleventh," 16.

31. M. Silver, *Economic,* 135.

32. Text available in A. Gardiner, *Late Egyptian Miscellanies* (Bruxelles, 1937), 103; the best published translation is in R. A. Caminos, *Late Egyptian Miscellanies* (Oxford, 1954), 304. Text quoted by Silver is from A. Blackman and T. E. Peet, "Papyrus Lansing: A Translation with Notes," *JEA* 11 (1925): 288.

33. Cf. the translation by R. A. Caminos, "The merchants fare downstream and upstream and are busy as brass, carrying goods ⟨from⟩ one town to another and supplying him that has not, although the tax-people *carry* gold, the most precious of all minerals," in R. A. Caminos, *Late,* 384, emphasis mine.

34. *Wörterbuch der Ägyptische Sprache,* vol. 1 (Leipzig, 1926–50),

572–73; *CDME,* 97.

35. In line 4:8–9, "The merchants . . . *f3y 3ḫt* ⟨*m*⟩ *niwt r kt,*" "carry goods ⟨from⟩ one city to another." In line 4:9–10, "the tax collectors *f3y nbw,*" "carry gold."

36. F. L. Griffith, "The Abydos Decree of Seti I at Nauri," *JEA* 13 (1927): 205. For a more recent discussion of the text, see A. Spalinger, "Some Revisions of Temple Endowments in the New Kingdom," *JARCE* 28 (1991): 21–40.

37. See lines 23 and 25, F. L. Griffith, "Abydos," 199.

38. See lines 30–33, F. L. Griffith, "Abydos," 200.

39. M. Silver, *Economic,* 76. No reference is cited.

40. J. W. Curtis, "Coinage in Pharaonic Egypt," *JEA* 43 (1957): 71–77.

41. J. Wilson in J. Pritchard, *Ancient Near Eastern Texts Relating to the Old Testament* (Princeton, 1969), 432.

42. H. Brunner, *Die Lehre des Cheti, Sohnes des Duauf* (Glückstadt and Hamburg, 1944), 31. On the numerous difficulties of this school text, see W. Helck, *Die Lehre des Dw3-ḫtjj,* vol. 1 (Wiesbaden, 1970).

43. Marquis of Northhampton, W. Spiegelberg, and P. E. Newberry, *Report on some Excavations in the Theban Necropolis* (London, 1908), pl. 8. A further reference in Louvre 421 omits *n Imn.* This stela is not published by either P. Pierret, *Recueil d'inscriptions inédites du Musée égyptien du Louvre* (Paris, 1874–78), or A. J. Gayet, *Musée du Louvre Stèles de la XIIe dynastie* (Paris, 1889). Both references are from H. Brunner, *Lehre,* 31.

44. For *bty* = "shepherd," see *Wb.* I 483:6. For *bṯy* quoted here see *Wb.* I 485:15–16, translated either as a profession in trade or a title. Brunner's solution is not entirely satisfactory. His translation is "Der Schafhirt (?) fahrt nach Norden ins Delta, um sich . . . zu holen. Nachdem er über seine Krafte viel geleistet hat bei der Arbeit und ihn die Mücken schon umgebraucht haben, plagen ihn noch die Sandfliegen und er wird. . . . " He does not translate *swn.*

45. W. Helck, *Lehre,* 49.

46. M. Silver, *Economic,* 135; text available in H. Gauthier, *La grande inscription dédicatoire d'Abydos* (Cairo, 1912). Translation available in H. Gauthier, "La grande inscription dédicatoire d'Abydos," *ZÄS* 48 (1911): 52–66. Text also available in *KRI,* vol. 2 (1979), 323–36.

47. *šwyt ḥr irt šwyt ḥr ḥnwt.sn b3kw.sn iry m nbw ḥmt.* For translation of *b3kw* as "temple dues," see E. Bleiberg, "Redistributive," 157–68.

48. For the convincing argument that all examples of such

šwty/šwyt are connected to institutions, see W. Reinecke, "Waren die *šwtyw* wirklich Kaufleute?" *AoF* 6 (1979): 5–14.

49. M. Silver, *Economic,* 135–36.

50. For the differences in writing, see *CDME,* 83.

51. *CDME,* 83.

52. M. Megally, *Le Papyrus hiératique comptable E. 3226 du Louvre* (Cairo, 1971), xxii, pl. vii. Cf. also A Recto, vi.2, xiii.

53. M. Silver, *Economic,* 136.

54. *Urk.* IV, 2145:4–6; translation available in W. Helck, *Urkunden der 18. Dynastie: Übersetzung zu den Heften* 17–22 (Berlin, 1961), 416–23.

55. *Urk.* IV 2143:15. Translation in W. Helck, *Urkunden,* 417.

56. M. Silver, *Economic,* 136.

57. R. A. Caminos, *Late,* 138.

58. Ibid., 137.

59. M. Silver, *Economic,* 136. T. Säve-Söderbergh, *The Navy of the Eighteenth Dynasty* (Uppsala, 1946), 61.

60. *P. Amiens,* 3:4.

61. A. Gardiner, "Ramesside Texts Relating to the Taxation and Transport of Corn," *JEA* 27 (1941): 47. My emphasis.

62. E. Castle, "Shipping and Trade in Ramesside Egypt," *JESHO* 35 (1992): 206–38. Thanks also to Stephen Vinson for sharing information from his forthcoming dissertation on first-millennium B.C. shipping.

63. "The ship's crews of every (commercial) house have received their load(s) (5:1) so that they may depart from Egypt to Djahy. Each man's god is with him. Not one of them dares say: 'We shall see Egypt (5:2) again.'" R. A. Caminos, *Late,* 304. M. Silver, *Economic,* 136.

64. On *P. Lansing* see R. A. Caminos, *Late,* 387. On the tomb robberies, see T. E. Peet, *The Great Tomb-robberies of the Twentieth Egyptian Dynasty,* vol. 1 (Oxford, 1930), 100n.18; see also Blackman and Peet, "Papyrus," 288n.13, and E. Wente in W. K. Simpson, ed., *The Literature of Ancient Egypt* (New Haven, 1973), 147 and n.1.

65. W. Helck, *Die Beziehungen Ägyptens zu Vorderasian im 3. und 2. Jahrtausend v. Chr. 2. verbesserte Auflage* (Wiesbaden, 1971), 431n.9.

66. Following E. Wente, in W. K. Simpson, ed., *Literature,* 147, quoted in M. Silver, *Economic,* 136.

67. W. Helck, *Beziehungen,* 431n.9.

68. B. Kemp, "Birth," 232–60.

69. Ibid., 233.

70. Ibid., 239.

71. Ibid., 240; even if the date of composition is Senwosret I's reign rather that just the date of deposition in Mesekh's tomb, the central government did not fully establish control of all resources until the "reforms" of Senwosret III.

72. Partially translated in *AEL,* vol. 1, 85–86; J. Vandier, *Mo'alla: La tombe d'Ankhtifi et la tombe de Sebekhotep* (Cairo, 1950). A complete translation is found in W. Schenkel, *Memphis, Herakleopolis, Theben* (Wiesbaden, 1965), no. 37, 45–57.

73. B. Kemp, "Birth," 253 ff.

74. Ibid., 246 ff.

75. Clearly visible in Kemp's reproduction of Newberry's plate. See B. Kemp, "Birth," fig. 84.

76. Kemp, "Birth," 244 ff.

77. For the original publication, see H. Frankfort and J. D. S. Pendlebury, *The City of Akhenaten,* part 2 (London, 1933), 59–61 and pl. 45.

78. B. Kemp, "Birth," 246.

79. T. E. Peet, "The Egyptian Words for 'Money,' 'Buy,' and 'Sell,' " in *Studies Presented to F. Ll. Griffith* (London, 1932), 124.

80. Biography of Harkhuf, *Urk.* I, 120–31. Translation in *AEL,* vol. 1, 23–27.

81. *Urk.* I, 124:9–15. "The majesty of Merenre sent me . . . to this foreign land. . . . I accomplished it in seven months having brought all the *inw* from there that I might be praised."

82. Following *AEL,* vol. 1, 114. For original text, see J. Couyat and P. Montet, *Les Inscriptions hiéroglyphiques et hiératiques du Ouâdi Hammâmât* (Cairo, 1912), 98–100, pl. 37.2.

83. The expedition is discussed in S. Ratié, *La reine Hatchepsout: Sources et problèmes* (Leiden, 1979), 139–61. The text is found in *Urk.* IV, 315–54.

84. A. Gardiner, *Late,* 61–76. Wenamun tried to act in a manner consistent with traditional royal trade. His report of his troubles demonstrates that this sort of trade could no longer exist without a strong central government. Though I have previously disputed Silver's use of Wenamun to show the existence of private merchants, the clear parallel of this opening statement with that of Harkhuf ("The Majesty of Merenre sent me . . . etc." *Urk.* I, 124:9–15) of the Old Kingdom shows that Wenamun was involved in the same commissioned trade that had already existed for thousands of years in Egypt.

85. Translation from *AEL,* vol. 2, 224.

86. J. W. Curtis, "Coinage," 71.

87. Ibid., 72.

88. P. Grierson, "Origins," 2.

89. Ibid., 8.

90. J. W. Curtis, "Media of Exchange in Ancient Egypt," *The Numismatist* (1951): 482–91; quoted in Curtis, "Coinage," 71.

91. A. Gardiner, "A Lawsuit Arising from the Purchase of Two Slaves," *JEA* 21 (1935): 140–46. J. Černý, "Prices and Wages in Egypt in the Ramesside Period," *Cahiers d'histoire mondiale* 1 (1951): 903–21. For silver as a synonym for payment, see S. Allam, "Silber = Leistung (in Form von beweglichen Vermogensgegenstande)," *Orientalia,* n.s. 36 (1967): 416–20. For many other examples of barter, see J. J. Janssen, *Commodity Prices from the Ramessid Period* (Leiden, 1975).

92. G. Dalton, *Economic Anthropology and Development* (London and New York, 1971), 64.

93. Major translations are "tribute" and "gift." *Wb.* I, 91:12–18; C. Aldred, "The Foreign Gifts Offered to Pharaoh," *JEA* 56 (1970): 111; R. Müller-Wollermann, "Bemerkungen," 81–93.

Chapter Two

1. P. Kaplony, *Die Inschriften der Ägyptischen Frühzeit,* vol. 1 (Wiesbaden, 1963), 292–97.

2. Gardiner Sign List (henceforth, G.S.L.) K.1 plus G.S.L. W.24 plus G.S.L. M.23. The group has also been understood as the name of a commodity in Z. Y. Saad, "Pottery Inscriptions," in W. Emery, *Tomb of Hor-Aha* (Cairo, 1939), 74–76.

3. P. Kaplony, *Inschriften,* vol. 2, 1005, Anm. 1609.

4. Ibid., vol. 1, 9; vol. 2, 1098, Abb. 36; vol. 3, Taf. 19, Abb. 36.

5. Ibid., vol. 3, Abb. II, nos. 210, 213, 214, 236, 281, 282, 847B.

6. J. Vandier, *Manuel,* vol. 1 (Paris, 1952), 597. For the rosette with the value *nsw,* see G. Bénédite, "The Carnarvon Ivory," *JEA* 5 (1918): 10. Most of the conventions of Egyptian writing had been established by this time; see A. J. Spencer, *Early Egypt: The Rise of Civilization in the Nile Valley* (London, 1993), 61–62; see also W. Helck, *Untersuchungen zur Thinitenzeit* (Wiesbaden, 1989), 139, no. 2, 141, no. 18, and S. Schott, "Hieroglyphen: Untersuchungen zum Ursprung der Schrift," *Akademie der Wissenschaften und der Literatur. Abhandlungen der Geistes- und Sozialwissenschaftlichen Klasse* 24 (1950), 20. Even if Schott's specific reading is not accepted, it seems clear that honorific

transposition was known by Narmer's time. See J. Kahl, *Das System der Ägyptischen Hieroglyphenschrift in der 0–3 Dynastie* (Wiesbaden, 1994), 97.

7. P. Kaplony, *Inschriften,* vol. 2 (1963), 994, Anm. 1586.

8. H. Junker, *Bericht über die Grabungen . . . auf dem Friedhof in Turah . . .* (Vienna, 1912), 7–9.

9. Berlin 18026, excavated by E. Amélineau, *Nouv. Fouilles* (Angers, 1897/98), pl. xv; A. Scharff, *Die Altertümer der Vor- und Frühzeit Ägyptens,* vol. 2, (Berlin, 1931), 171, No. 336; V. Vikentiev, "Les Monuments archaïques VI," *BIÉ* 36 (1954): 297, fig. 4B; W. Kaiser, *Ägyptisches Museum Berlin* (Berlin, 1967), 18, no. 161; A. Gordon, "Context," 65. The transcriptions of royal names in Dyn. 1 follow those devised by K. Baer and published by M. Hoffman, *Egypt Before the Pharaohs* (Austin, 1991), 270.

10. Berlin 15, 499. Discovered by W. M. F. Petrie. A. Scharff, *Altertümer,* vol. 2, 171 no. 337.

11. M. Hoffman, *Egypt,* 285; H. S. Smith, "Walter Bryan Emery," *JEA* 57 (1971): 199; B. Kemp, "Abydos and the Royal Tombs of the First Dynasty," *JEA* 52 (1966): 13–22.

12. Conveniently described in M. Hoffman, *Egypt,* 268.

13. J. Garstang, "The Tablet of Mena," *ZÄS* 42 (1905): 61, figs. 1 and 2.; A. Gordon, "Context," 64. On the identification of the tomb owner, see P. Kaplony, *Inschriften,* vol. 1 (1963), 68, and W. Helck, "Naqada," *LdÄ* 4 (1980): 344–46.

14. P. Kaplony, *Inschriften,* vol. 3 (1963) pl. 147, no. 849. Cf. W. Emery, *Hor-Aha* (1939), pl. 20, nos. 196–202; pls. 14–22, nos. 1–34, 36, 86, 81, 93, 105–25.

15. W. Emery, *Great Tombs,* vol. 2 (1954), 102–03, pl. xxxvb; A. Gordon, "Context," 66.

16. V. Vikentiev, "Études d'épigraphie protodynastiques," *ASAE* 56 (1959): 6 fig. 1; A. Gordon, "Context," 67.

17. W. Emery, *Great Tombs,* vol. 3 (1958), pl. 107, no. 18, cf. pl. 107, nos. 20 and 22.

18. P. Kaplony, *Inschriften* vol. 1, 11; vol. 2, 1107; vol. 3, pl. 34.

19. JE 70114; W. Emery, *Tomb of Hemaka* (Cairo, 1936), 35–36, pl. 17A.; A. Gordon, "Context," 65; *PM* III^2, 440; B. Grdseloff, "Notes sur deux Monuments inédits de l'Ancien Empire," *ASAE* 42 (1943): 112–14, fig. 17; V. Vikentiev, "Les Monuments archaïques IV–V," *BIÉ* 32 (1949–50): 189, pl. i[6], fig. 7; I. Gamer-Wallert, *Fische und Fischkulte im Alten Ägypten,* Taf. xiii[2].

20. R. Macramallah, *Un cimetière archaïque de la classe moyenne du*

peuple à Saqqarah (Cairo, 1940), 66, pl. 47; see also page 22.

21. See examples in chapter 3 from P. Boulaq 18.

22. A. Roth, *Egyptian Phyles in the Old Kingdom* (Chicago, 1991), 1.

23. G.S.L. W.25. For the sign see A. Scharff, *Archäologische Beiträge zur Frage der Entstehung der Hieroglyphenschrift* (Hildesheim, 1975), 72.

24. E. Ayrton, *Abydos,* vol. 3 (London, 1904), pl. ix, no. 1.

25. E. Naville, *Cemeteries of Abydos,* vol. 1 (London, 1914), pl. x; A. Gordon, "Context," 69; P. Kaplony, *Inschriften,* vol. 2, 787, and 1131 where he translated *Sṯt* as the name of a "city of Asians" located in the Delta.

26. P. Lacau and J. Ph. Lauer, *La Pyramide à degrés,* vol. 4 (Cairo, 1959), pl. 18, no. 87; cf. P. Kaplony, *Beschriftete Kleinfunde . . .* (Istanbul, 1973), pl. 8, no. 28.

27. P. Kaplony, *Steingefässe mit Inschriften* (Bruxelles, 1968), 39–40, n.18; A. Gordon, "Context," 70.

28. For example, W. M. F. Petrie, *Royal Tombs of the Earliest Dynasties,* vol. 2 (London, 1901), pl. 22, no. 190.

29. Suggested to me by D. B. Redford. On Dynasty 2 burials in Saqqara, see A. J. Spencer, *Early,* 84.

30. For the Dynasty 4 Overseer of *wab*-priests of Peribsen, Sheri, see *PM* III[2,] 490; A. Mariette, *Les Mastabas de l'Ancien Empire* (Hildesheim, 1976), 92–93; L. Borchardt, *Denkmäler des Alten Reiches,* vol. 1 (Berlin, 1937), 42–44, bl. 10. Thanks to Betsy Bryan for this reference.

31. See P. Kaplony, *Inschriften,* vol. 1, 158; vol. 2, 1002; P. Kaplony, *Steingefässe,* 40; A. Gordon, "Context," 69.

32. E. Bleiberg, "Commodity," 107–10; E. Bleiberg, "Kings," 155–67.

33. P. Lauer and J-Ph. Lacau, *Pyramide,* vol. 5 (1965), 36.

34. Ibid., 38, no. 57, pl. 24:6, 7.

35. Ibid., 45, no. 81, pl. 27:7.

36. Ibid., 65, no. 158, fig. 109.

37. Ibid., 56, no. 159, fig. 110.

38. Ibid., 71, no. 181. The little-understood title *mitr* occurs also in no. 51, pl. 37, and at Giza in H. Junker, *Giza,* vol. 12 (Vienna, 1944), 170; see also W. Helck, *Untersuchungen,* 267, no. 8, for the translation "palace worker."

39. P. Lauer and J-Ph. Lacau, *Pyramide,* vol. 5 (1965), 72, no. 184, fig. 133.

40. Ibid., 56, no. 131, figs. 82a, b, c.

41. Ibid., 56, no. 133, fig. 83.

42. Ibid., 57, no. 134, fig. 84.

43. Ibid., 13, no. 17, fig. 21.

44. Ibid., 40, no. 67; A. Gordon, "Context," 74.

45. P. Lauer and J-Ph. Lacau, *Pyramide,* vol. 5 (1965), 54, no. 123, pl. 33:4.

46. Ibid., 21, no. 31, fig. 31.

47. Ibid., 36, no. 48: A. Gordon, "Context," 73.

48. P. Lauer and J-Ph. Lacau, *Pyramide,* vol. 5 (1965), 74, no. 194, fig. 142.

49. Ibid., 40, no. 64; A. Gordon, "Context," 72.

50. P. Lauer and J-Ph. Lacau, *Pyramide,* vol. 5 (1965), 6; A. Gordon, "Context," 70.

51. P. Lauer and J-Ph. Lacau, *Pyramide,* vol. 5 (1965), 1; A. Gordon, "Context," 73.

52. Searches of the literature have not revealed any examples of *inw* from Dynasty 4.

53. *Urk.* I, 240:2–5; on the suggestion that this is a Dyn. 25 copy, see W. Helck, *Geschichte des Alten Ägypten* (Leiden, 1968), 28n.2.

54. P. Posener-Kriéger and J. L. de Cénival, eds., *Abu-Sir* (1968), pl. 45c.

55. W. K. Simpson, *Hekanefer and the Dynastic Material from Toshka and Arminna* (New Haven and Philadelphia, 1963), fig. 40, pl. xxvb; A. Gordon, "Context," 61.

56. *Urk.* I, 149:16–17; this translation and transcription ignores K. Sethe's unnecessary emendation of the text from *nsw* to *šmꜥw.* See J. Couyat and P. Montet, *Inscriptions,* 31 and pl. 35.

57. K. Sethe, *PT,* vol. 2 (1910), p. 317, line 1499, Spell 575; A. Gordon, "Context," 62.

58. *Urk.* I, 123:15–124:1.

59. Ibid., 124:9–15.

60. Ibid., 124:17–125:7.

61. Ibid., 128:9–11.

62. Ibid., 139:3–6.

63. P. Posener-Kriéger and J. L. de Cénival, *Abu-Sir,* pl. 95A, b4; A. Gordon, "Context," 75.

64. P. Posener-Kriéger and J. L. de Cénival, *Abu-Sir,* pl. 62, line 47: A. Gordon, "Context," 75.

65. P. Posener-Kriéger and J. L. de Cénival, *Abu-Sir,* pl. 62; A. Gordon, "Context," 74.

66. For the largely unheeded pleas not to translate *inw* as "tribute," see most recently R. Müller-Wollermann, "Bemerkungen,"

81–93.

67. P. Posener-Kriéger, *Les Archives du temple funéraire de Néferirka-rê-Kakaï (Les Papyrus d'Abousir)*, vol. 1 (Cairo, 1976), 313; translation mine.

68. P. Posener-Kriéger and J. L. de Cénival, *Abu-Sir*, pl. 52A, 3C; A. Gordon, "Context," 74.

69. *LD* ii, 42; S. Hassan, *Excavations*, vol. 4 (Cairo, 1932–33), 103, 23, fig. 58; *PM* III, 233.

70. N. de G. Davies, *The Mastabah of Ptahhetep and Akhethetep at Saqqara*, vol. 1 (London, 1901), xxi; R. F. E. Paget and A. A. Pirie, *The Tomb of Ptahhetep* (London, 1989), pls. 31 and 33; A. Gordon, "Context," 53 ff.

71. N. de G. Davies, *Mastabah*, vol. 2 (1901), pls. xiii, xiv, xv.

72. H. Jacquet-Gordon, *Les Noms des Domaines funéraires sous l'Ancien Empire égyptien* (Cairo, 1962), 19.

73. Y. Harpur, *Decoration in Egyptian Tombs of the Old Kingdom* (London, 1987), 236.

74. Ibid., 227.

75. Ibid.

76. For identifications see S. Hassan, *Excavations*, vol. 4 (1932–33), 112–13.

77. As A. Gordon has observed, *inw* cannot be a participle describing *nḏt-ḥr* because in that case the feminine participle *int* would be required ("Context," 53).

78. See Y. Harpur, *Decoration*, 221.

79. W. Helck, "Thothfest," *LdÄ* (1985): 523.

80. Most recently, A. Roth, *Egyptian*, 69–70; J. Capart, "Note sur un fragment de bas-relief au British Museum," *BIFAO* 30 (1931): 74; A. Erman, *Reden Rufe u. Lieder auf Gräberbildern des Alten Reiches* (Berlin, 1919), 60.

81. On *ᶜḳw* (regular provisions) see P. Posener-Kriéger, *Archives*, vol. 1, 222n.1. On *ḥtp-nṯr* (goods from the *pr-nsw*), see P. Posener-Kriéger, *Archives*, vol. 1, 619. On *3wt* (goods from the *Ḫnw*), see P. Posener-Kriéger, *Archives*, vol. 1, 332–33.

82. Tomb of Nesu-nefer, H. Junker, *Giza*, vol. 3 (1938), 183, 184; Tomb of Nebkawher, Hassan and Iskander, *Giza*, vol. 1 (1929), 49; Hassan and Iskander, *Giza*, vol. 2 (1930–31), 49; Tomb of Idut, Junker, *Giza*, vol. 3 (1938), 112.

Chapter Three

1. Other typically royal prerogatives found in provincial rulers' tombs include the symbolism of the papyrus and lotus plant uniting Upper and Lower Egypt; women depicted performing agricultural tasks normally done by men; processions of fecundity figures; and wearing the the Bat emblem. See D. Franke, "The Career of Khnumhotep III of Beni Hasan and the So-Called 'Decline of the Nomarchs,' " in S. Quirke, ed., *Middle Kingdom Studies* (New Malden, 1991), 54 ff.

2. A. Volten, *Zwei altägyptische politische Schriften: Die Lehre für König Merikare und die Lehre des Königs Amenemhet* (Copenhagen, 1945), 39, l. 75; A. Gordon, "Context," 96–97 (from *P. Hermitage* 1116A dating to the reign of Amenhotep II). Text also available in W. Helck, *Lehre*, 46. Perhaps the text actually dates to Dynasty 12.

3. H. Brunner, *Die Texte aus den Gräbern der Herakleopolitenzeit von Siut* (Glückstadt, 1937), 44:11; A. Gordon, "Context," 78.

4. A. Blackman, "The Stele of Thethi, Brit. Mus. No. 614," *JEA* 17 (1931): pl. 8, ll. 4–6; A. Gordon, "Context," 79.

5. J. Couyat and P. Montet, *Inscriptions*, 82, l.9–83,1:15; on foreign expeditions during the Middle Kingdom, see K-J. Seyfried, *Beiträge zu den Expeditionen des Mittleren Reiches in die Ost-Wüste* (Hildesheim, 1981), n.b. 281, where it is clear that this particular expedition is the only one in this period to call the goods brought back *inw.*

6. H. Altenmüller and A. Moussa, "Die Inschrift Amenemhets II aus den Ptah Tempel von Memphis: Ein Vorbericht," SAK *18* (1991): 18, and *Falttafel* 1, ll 24–25. See also G. Posener, "A New Inscription of the XIIth Dynasty," *JSSEA* 12 (1982): 7–8. On *Wḥ*ᶜ*-Nbty*, see R. A. Caminos, *Literary Fragments in the Hieratic Script* (Oxford, 1956), pls. 9 and 11. See also *Urk.* IV, 158:4.

7. P. Newberry, *Beni Hasan*, vol. 2 (London, 1893), pl. xxxii; A. Gordon, "Context," 81. For comments on the dating of the tomb, see note 13 below.

8. A. Blackman, *The Rock Tombs of Meir*, vol. 1, (London, 1914), pl. ix; A. Gordon, "Context," 84.

9. A. Blackman, *Meir*, vol. 1 (1914), pl. iii; A. Gordon, "Context," 83–84.

10. A. Blackman, *Meir*, vol. 2 (1915), pl. ii; A. Gordon, "Context," 89.

11. A. Blackman, *Meir*, vol. 2 (1915), pl. xiii; A. Gordon, "Context," 89.

12. A. Blackman, *Meir,* vol. 2 (1915), pl. xi; A. Gordon, "Context," 84.

13. The relative chronology of Beni Hasan Tombs 29, 33, and 15 is undisputed. P. Newberry dated all three tombs to Dynasty 11. W. Schenkel redated Tomb 15, belonging to Baqet III, to the reign of Amenemhet I on paleographic grounds. See his *Frühmittelägyptische Studien* (Bonn, 1962). This dating is most recently accepted by H. O. Willems, "The Nomarchs of the Hare Nome and early Middle Kingdom History," *JEOL* 28 (1985): 80–102, n.b. 92 ff. D. Spanel has questioned the dating, placing all three tombs as early as Dynasty 9 in "Beni Hasan in the Herakleopolitan Period" (unpublished Ph.D. dissertation, University of Toronto, 1984). L. Gestermann has dated two tombs to late Dynasty 11 (Tombs 29 and 33 in the reign of Mentuhotep IV) and the tomb of Baqet III as late as the reign of Senwosret I. See L. Gestermann, *Kontinuität und Wandel in Politik und Verwaltung des Früh Mittleren Reiches in Ägypten* (Wiesbaden, 1987), 187. C. Hölzl maintains similar dates on architectural grounds. See his "Studien zu Entwicklung der Felsengräber: Datierung und lockale Entwicklung der Felsengräber des Mittleren Reiches in Mittelägypten." (unpublished Ph.D. dissertation, University of Vienna, n.d.). The absolute chronology of these tombs is important to a discussion of *inw* only insofar as it clarifies the relationship between the central authority and local rulers.

14. A. Blackman, *Meir,* vol. 1 (1914), pl. iii.

15. Tomb of Merire, N. de G. Davies, *The Rock Tombs of el Amarna,* vol. 2 (London, 1905), pl. 38 and H. H. Nelson et al., *Later Historical Records of Rameses III: Medinet Habu,* vol. 2 (Chicago, 1932), pl. 111. See also A. D. Touney and S. Wenig, *Der Sport im Alten Ägypten* (Leipzig, 1969), pl. 6. Wrestling is also shown as part of military training. See, for example, at Beni Hasan Tomb 2 (*Beni Hasan,* vol. 1, pls. 14, 15, 16), Tomb 15 (*Beni Hasan,* vol. 2, pls. 5, 8), and Tomb 17 (*Beni Hasan,* vol. 2, pl. 15). A third very fragmentary Middle Kingdom scene might link the phrase *inw n sẖt* with a wrestling scene, but this is conjectural because the fragments do not certainly come from the same scene. See Tomb of Nehri, P. Newberry, *El Bersheh,* vol. 2 (London, 1893–94), pl. 11. On wrestling, see W. Decker, "Neue Dokumente zum Ringkampf in alten Ägypten," *Kölner Beiträge zur Sportwissenschaft* 5 (1976): 7–24; W. Decker, "Ringen," *LdÄ* 5 (1984): 265–66; W. Decker, *Sports and Games of Ancient Egypt* (New Haven, 1992), 72–82.

16. P. Newberry, *Beni Hasan,* vol. 2 (London, 1893), pl. xxviii.

17. Ibid., pl. xxxv; A. Gordon, "Context," 81.

18. Perhaps personified as Sekhet, see W. Guglielmi, *Sechat, LdÄ,* vol. 5, 778; W. Guglielmi, "Die Feldgöttin *Sḫt,*" *Die Welt des Orients* 7 (1974): 206–27.

19. Reproduced in Y. Harpur, *Decoration,* fig. 83.

20. Altenmüller and Moussa, "Inschrift," 18, and the above section in chapter 3 entitled "Traditional Exchanges of *Inw* for the King at Thebes in Dynasty 11."

21. P. Newberry, *Beni Hasan,* vol. 1 (London, 1893), pl. 8; *Urk.* VII, 14:10–19; D. Lorton, "The So-called 'Vile' Enemies of the King of Egypt," *JARCE* 10 (1973): 6; A. Gordon, "Context," 87.

22. *Urk.* VII, 1–2; A. Gardiner, "Inscriptions from the tomb of Si-renpowet, Prince of Elephantine." *ZÄS* 45 (1908): 4–5, pl. vii; A. Gordon, "Context," 85; D. Lorton, *The Juridical Terminology of International Relations in Egyptian Texts through Dyn. XVIII* (Baltimore, 1974), 157n.26.

23. P. Newberry, *El Bersheh,* vol. 1 (1895), pl. 27; A. Gordon, "Context," 93.

24. P. Newberry, *Beni Hasan,* vol. 2 (1893), pl. vii; A. Gordon, "Context," 80.

25. P. Newberry, *Beni Hasan,* vol. 1 (1893), pl. xx; A. Gordon, "Context," 83.

26. P. Newberry, *Beni Hasan,* vol. 1 (1893), pl. xviii; A. Gordon, "Context," 88.

27. P. Newberry, *Beni Hasan,* vol. 1 (1893), pl. xvii; A. Gordon, "Context," 87. Note the reversal of the walking legs here.

28. P. Newberry, *Beni Hasan,* vol. 2 (1893), pl. xxiv; A. Gordon, "Context," 94.

29. P. Newberry, *Beni Hasan,* vol. 1 (1893), pl. xxvi, 150–54; A. Gordon, "Context," 90.

30. P. Newberry, *Beni Hasan,* vol. 1 (1893), pl. xxx; A. Gordon, "Context," 90.

31. P. Newberry, *El Bersheh,* vol. 1 (1895), pl. xx; A. Gordon, "Context," 92.

32. A. Blackman, *Meir,* vol. 6 (1953), pl. xviii; A. Gordon, "Context," 91.

33. A. Blackman, *Meir,* vol. 6 (1953), pl. xviii; A. Gordon, "Context," 90–91.

34. I am grateful to Betsy M. Bryan for this suggestion.

35. For bibliography, see *PM* IV[1], 145 (7)–(11). For additional bibliography, see H. Goedicke, "Abi-Shai's Representation in Beni

Hasan," *JARCE* 21 (1984): 203. A very interesting addition to this literature is found in D. Kessler, "Die Asiatenkarawane von Beni Hassan," *SAK* 14 (1987): 147–65.

36. D. Kessler, "Asiatenkarawane," 158.

37. P. Newberry, *El Bersheh,* vol. 1 (1895), pl. xx.

38. J. Baines, *Fecundity Figures: Egyptian Personification and the Iconology of a Genre* (Chicago, 1985), 156–57.

39. D. Franke, in S. Quirke, ed., *Middle,* 54.

40. N. Davies, *Ptahhetep and Akhethotep* (London, 1900–1901), pl. 14.

41. F. L. Griffith, *The Petrie Papyri: Hieratic Papyri from Kahun and Gurob* (London, 1898).

42. At this writing the archive is being prepared for publication by Stephen Quirke. The archive is preserved at the Ägyptisches Museen in Berlin. An incomplete set of transcriptions made by Eugène Dévaud is preserved at the Griffith Institute in the Gardiner archives. These transcriptions include marginal notes in German by an unknown hand. A letter dated 1955 in the Gardiner archive of the Griffith Institute (AHG.30.194c) reveals that Gardiner obtained these copies of Dévaud's work from Grapow, who was at that time responsible for the publication of the archive. Further helpful information on these documents is found in the catalog assembled by U. Kaplony-Heckel, *Ägyptische Handschriften,* vol. 1 (Wiesbaden, 1971). The following transliterations are based on Dévaud's transcriptions and some limited checking against the original papyri. The author gratefully acknowledges the kindness of Jaromir Málek, who enabled access to the Gardiner archive in the Griffith Institute, Ashmolean Museum, Oxford, and of Ingeborg Müller, who arranged access to the papyri during a June 1990 visit to Berlin.

43. B. Kemp, *Ancient Egypt: Anatomy of a Civilization* (London, 1989), 149.

44. F. L. Griffith, *Petrie,* pl. 16 (= P. Kahun VI:10); Gordon, "Context," 101. S. Quirke, *The Administration of Egypt in the Late Middle Kingdom: The Hieratic Documents* (New Malden, 1990), 153 n.30, 165, 182n.40. On the reading *kmt.n.f* versus *kmt n.f,* see A. Spalinger, "Notes on the Day Summary Accounts of P. Boulaq 18," *SAK* 12 (1985): 203n.34, and "Foods in P. Boulaq 18," *SAK* 13 (1986): 221–22.

45. A. Scharff, "Ein Rechnungsbuch des Königlichen Hofes aus der 13. Dynastie," *ZÄS* 57 (1922): 5**, S12 (= P. Boulaq 18, XVIII, 1:4); S. Quirke, *Administration,* 33n.39, 43, 46n.1, 47n.5, 48n.9.

46. A. Scharff, "Rechnungsbuch," 8**, S25 (= P. Boulaq 18, XXI, 2:1); A. Gordon, "Context," 107; S. Quirke, *Administration,* 33n.39, 46n.1, 98n.1, 109; A. Spalinger, "Notes," 180–91. Scharff dated the text to the reign of Sobekhotep III. Quirke believes it to date to the reign of Sobekhotep II.

47. A. Scharff, "Rechnungsbuch," 20**, S68 (= P. Boulaq 18, XLIII, 3); Fr. W. v. Bissing, "Miscellen," *ZÄS* 40 (1902): 96; S. Quirke, *Administration,* 112; for the title see W. Ward, *Index of Egyptian Administrative and Religious Titles of the Middle Kingdom* (Beirut, 1982), No. 1087.

48. A. Scharff, "Rechnungsbuch," 15**, S55 (= P. Boulaq 18, XXXII, 1–2); S. Quirke, *Administration,* 26n.11, 28n.19, 42–43, 51, 58–59, 61–64, 94; A. Spalinger, "Foods," 226; Quirke sees this passage as evidence of *inw* moving from the palace to individuals. Spalinger interprets this line as *inw* moving from these individuals to the palace.

49. A. Scharff, "Rechnungsbuch," 14**, S49 (= P. Boulaq 18, XXX, 2:5); S. Quirke, *Administration,* 46.

50. A. Scharff, "Rechnungsbuch," 11**, S39 (= P. Boulaq 18, XXVII, 18–19); S. Quirke, *Administration,* 64, 111; R. J. Leprohon, "Some Remarks on the 'Administrative Department' (*wꜥrt*) of the Late Middle Kingdom," *JSSEA* 10 (1980): 164. On *ẖ3 dd rmt* translated as "Bureau of the People's Giving," see S. Quirke, *Administration,* 110, 112.

51. A. Scharff, "Rechnungsbuch," 10**, S34 (= P. Boulaq 18, XXV, 2:16); S. Quirke, *Administration,* 26n.11, 59, 64, 98n.1, 111, 121.

52. A. Scharff, "Rechnungsbuch," 3**, S10 (= P. Boulaq 18, XV, 4:1) and 9**, S34 (= P. Boulaq 18, XXV, 2:1); S. Quirke, *Administration,* 26n.11, 30n.28, 32n.32, 59, 64, 98n.1, 111, 121; A. Spalinger, *SAK* 12 (1985): 199–200; A. Spalinger, "Notes," 211–13; R. J. Leprohon, "Some Remarks," 163.

53. W. C. Hayes, "Notes on the Government of Egypt in the Late Middle Kingdom," *JNES* 12 (1953): 31–39, is an important statement of the role of the new government departments. Hayes is concerned with *Wilbour Papyrus* 35.1446, but his comments are certainly relevant here. See also H. Kees, "Zur Bedeutung vom *wꜥrt* in Urkunden der M.R.," *ZÄS* 70 (1934): 86–91.

54. S. Quirke, *Administration,* 110.

55. Ibid., 123.

56. P. Berlin 10,041r (AHG.30.232.1); U. Kaplony-Heckel, *Ägyptische,* no. 31.

57. P. Berlin 10,041r (AHG.30.232.1); U. Kaplony-Heckel, *Agyptische,* no. 31.

58. P. Berlin 10,044e (AHG.30.235.6); U. Kaplony-Heckel, *Agyptische,* no. 317 (Inv. no. P. Berlin 10,224e).

59. P. Berlin 10,045c (AHG.30.236.5); U. Kaplony-Heckel, *Agyptische,* no. 73 (Inv. no. P. Berlin 10,089b).

60. P. Berlin 10,045a (AHG.30.236.2); U. Kaplony Heckel, *Agyptische,* no. 74 (Inv. no. P. Berlin 10,089c).

61. U. Kaplony-Heckel, *Agyptische,* (1971), no. 275 (Inv. no. P. Berlin 10,224).

62. P. Berlin 10,006 (AHG.30.199.1); U. Kaplony-Heckel, *Agyptische,* no. 5.

63. P. Berlin 10,077 (AHG.30.268.1); U. Kaplony-Heckel, *Agyptische,* no. 60.

64. P. Berlin 10,009r (AHG.30.201.1); U. Kaplony-Heckel, *Agyptische,* no. 7.

65. P. Berlin 10,092 (AHG. 30.283.3); U. Kaplony-Heckel, *Agyptische,* no. 78.

66. P. Berlin 10,007 (AHG.30.200); U. Kaplony-Heckel, *Agyptische,* no. 6.

67. U. Kaplony-Heckel, *Agyptische,* 25–26, no. 44. (= P. Berlin 10,056A); Dévaud's transcription = AHG.30.247.1.

68. U. Kaplony-Heckel, *Agyptische,* 105 (= P. Berlin 10,203). Cf. P. Berlin 10,003r (AHG.30.196.1), which joins this fragment.

69. P. Berlin 10,055 (AHG.30.246.3). For conjectural restoration, cf. P. Berlin 10,056A. Kaplony-Heckel, *Agyptische,* no. 43.

70. P. Berlin 10,002Ar (AHG.30.195.10); U. Kaplony-Heckel, *Agyptische,* no. 2.

71. U. Kaplony-Heckel, *Agyptische,* 230 (= P. Berlin 10,397, fragment 585).

72. F. L. Griffith, *Petrie,* pl. 26, (= P. Kahun LV.8); A. Gordon, "Context," 103; on *b3kw,* see C. Eyre, "An Accounts Papyrus from Thebes," *JEA* 66 (1980): 108–19; E. Bleiberg, "Redistributive," 157–68. S. Quirke, *Administration,* 165, 181n.34.

73. F. L. Griffith, *Petrie,* pl. 15 (= P. Kahun XLIV.1); A. Gordon, "Context," 103; S. Quirke, *Administration,* 184 n.54.

74. F. L. Griffith, *Petrie,* pl. 26, (= P. Kahun IX.1).

75. A. Scharff, "Rechnungsbuch," 2**, S7 (= P. Boulaq 18 XV.2: 14–18); A. Gordon, "Context," 104; S. Quirke, *Administration,* 34n.43, 43, 47n.6, 103, 105; A. Spalinger, "Foods," 223.

76. A. Scharff, "Rechnungsbuch," 3**, S9 (= P. Boulaq 18 XV.3:1–

2); A. Gordon, "Context," 106; S. Quirke, *Administration,* 30n.27, 40; A. Spalinger, "Foods," 223–24.

77. A. Scharff, "Rechnungsbuch," 9**, S33 (= P. Boulaq 18 XXIV:18–19); S. Quirke, *Administration,* 85n.4; A. Spalinger, "Foods," 225.

78. A. Scharff, "Rechnungsbuch," 11**, S37 (= P. Boulaq 18 XXVI:7–10); A. Gordon, "Context," 105; S. Quirke, *Administration,* 43, 102; A. Spalinger, "Foods," 225.

79. A. Scharff, "Rechnungsbuch," 14**, S48 (= P. Boulaq 18 XXX:1); S. Quirke, *Administration,* 98n.2, 111, 119; A. Spalinger, "Notes," 203n.34; A. Spalinger, "Foods," 221–22.

80. S. Quirke, *Administration,* 110.

81. A. Spalinger, "Notes," 179–241, n.b. 192–200.

82. A. Blackman, *Middle Egyptian Stories* (Bruxelles, 1932), 74, ll. 174–75; A. Gordon, "Context," 97.

83. A. Blackman, (Bruxelles, 1932), 24, l. B8; Gordon, 100.

84. A. Gardiner, *The Admonitions of an Egyptian Sage* (Hildesheim, 1969), 3, 6–8; A. Gordon, "Context," 99.

85. F. Vogelsang, *Kommentar zu den Klagen des Bauern* (Leipzig, 1913) (= Peas. 29–30 ll. R7–35); A. Gordon, "Context," 97; R. B. Parkinson, *The Tale of the Eloquent Peasant* (Oxford, 1991), 1–6, ll. 1.7–6.1.

Chapter Four

This chapter appeared in a different version as "The King's Privy Purse during the New Kingdom," *JARCE* 21 (1984): 155–67. Changes and additions have been made due to additional study of the earlier periods. This chapter has also benefited from J. J. Janssen's comments in his essay "*b3kw*: From Work to Product," *SAK* 20 (1993): 81–94. M. Liverani, *Prestige and Interest* (Padua, 1990), 255–67, came to my attention too late to be considered here.

1. *Urk.* IV, 248:5–8.
2. C. Zivie, *Giza au deuxième millénaire* (Cairo, 1976), 128:15.
3. *Urk.* IV, 1656:5–10.
4. *KRI* I, 26:9 ff; see similar ll. 11, 13, and 30:11.
5. W. Erichsen, *P. Harris,* 66b:7.
6. E. Bleiberg, "Commodity," 107 ff.
7. *Urk.* IV, 76:15–16.
8. Ibid., 83:9–10.

9. Ibid., 138:3–4.
10. Ibid., 326:2–3.
11. Ibid., 1235:3–13.
12. Ibid., 1326:1–5.
13. A. Shorter, "Historical Scarabs of Thuthmosis IV and Amenophis III," *JEA* 17 (1931): 23, fig. 1.
14. *Urk.* IV, 1693:8–14.
15. For example, A. Brack, *Das Grab des Tjanuni* (Mainz, 1977), 40, pl. 331.
16. For examples of *inw* translated as a gift, see E. Blumenthal, *Untersuchungen zu Ägyptischen Königtum des Mittleren Reiches,* vol. 1 (Berlin, 1970), 194. For gift-giving as an economic institution among common people in Egypt, see J. J. Janssen, "Gift Giving in Ancient Egypt as an Economic Feature," *JEA* 68 (1982): 253–58.
17. See M. Mauss, *The Gift* (London, 1954); C. Zaccagnini, *Lo scambio dei doni nel vicino oriente durante i secoli xv–xiii* (Rome, 1973).
18. D. Forde and M. Douglas, "Primitive Economics," in G. Dalton, ed., *Tribal and Peasant Economies* (Garden City, N.Y., 1967), 23.
19. *Urk.* IV, 1235:3–5.
20. Ibid., 658, 663.
21. *In-r-t, Urk.* IV, 690; Naharain, *Urk.* IV, 711; *In-iw-ks, Urk.* IV, 716; and Tunip, *Urk.* IV, 730.
22. Retenu, *Urk.* IV, 668 and passim; Wartjet, *Urk.* IV, 686; Assyria, *Urk.* IV, 668, 671, 726 [?]; Genbut, *Urk.* IV, 695; Sengar, *Urk.* IV, 700; Hatti, *Urk.* IV, 701, 726.
23. For a Mesopotamian view of diplomatic relations as family relations and thus hierarchical, see J. M. Munn-Rankin, "Diplomacy in Western Asia in the Early Second Millennium, B.C." *Iraq* 18 (1956): 68–110, esp. 76 ff.
24. *Wb.* II, 369:2–7; R. Faulkner, *CDME,* 143; A. M. Bakir, *Slavery in Pharaonic Egypt* (Cairo, 1952), 38–41; D. Lorton, *Juridical,* 115–17.
25. *Urk.* IV, 1247:7–8.
26. See references in the table on pages 94–95.
27. *Urk.* IV, 1821:5–9.
28. Burnaburiah: EA 6:13–16, 61, 64–65; 9:15–18; 10:16–17; 11:19–23. Asshuruballat: EA 16:32–34. Tushratta: EA 19:66–70. Suppiluliuma: EA 41:16–22. Cyprus: EA 35:19–21; 37:16–18.
29. EA 17:36–45; 18Rs:1–4; 19:80–85; 20:20–84: 21:33–38: 22; 25; 26:64–66 [for Ty]; 27:110–14; 29:182–89.
30. *Urk.* IV, 668:17 ff.

31. W. Hayes, "The Inscriptions from the Palace of Amenhotep III," *JNES* 10 (1951): 32, 82, 156, 231. For O'Connor's discoveries, see M. A. Leahy, *Excavations at Malkatta: The Inscriptions* (Warminster, 1978).

32. E. Dziobek, *Das Grab des Ineni: Theben Nr. 81.* (Mainz, 1992), 33–34.

33. *Urk.* IV, 867:16.

34. Ibid., 1253:3.

35. Ibid., 1651:16–1652:1.

36. *KRI* I, 10:11; similar 15:8 ff; 19:9 ff; 23:3 ff.

37. *KRI* II, 143:11 ff; similar, 146:10; 147:9; 154:10; 156:8; 167:7; 207:13.

38. P. Harris, 8:3.

39. Ibid., 13a:3; similar 33a:3; 52a:6; 62b:3; 70a:5.

40. Ibid., 26:12.

41. P. Harris 49:6; similar 59:9.

42. J. J. Janssen, *Commodity Prices from the Ramessid Period* (Leiden, 1975), 456. I would also like to thank A. Roccati, who made it possible for me to examine this papyrus in 1981.

43. *Urk.* IV, 983:16–984:6.

44. A. Brack, *Tjanuni* (Mainz, 1977), 40, pl. 31.

45. *Urk.* IV, 953:16–954:5.

46. G. Martin, *The Memphite Tomb of Horemheb, Commander in Chief of Tutankhamun,* vol. 1 (London, 1989), pl. 91.

47. A. Gardiner, *Late,* (Bruxelles, 1937), 120.

48. C. Aldred, "Year Twelve at el-Amarna," *JEA* 43 (1957): 114; *ARE* §1027; R. O. Faulkner, "The Wars of Sethos I," *JEA* 33 (1947): 34. See also C. Aldred, "Foreign," 112 ff.

49. C. Aldred, "Foreign," 114.

50. For the text, see A. Gardiner, "A Pharaonic Encomium," *JEA* 41 (1955): pl. vii.

51. D. B. Redford, *History and Chronology of the Eighteenth Dynasty: Seven Studies* (Toronto, 1967), 120–28.

52. *Urk.* IV, 153:16.

53. *PM* I.1^{2,} 42 (8).

54. *Urk.* IV, 953:13–14.

55. *PM* I.1^{2} 170, (16); M. M. A. photo T. 1874–75.

56. H. Guksch, *Das Grab des Benja, gen. Paheqamen: Theben Nr 343* (Mainz, 1978), pl. 9.

57. *Urk.* IV, 1115:4.

58. *PM* I.1^{2} (1960), 42 (8).

59. *PM* I.1² (1960), 170, and M. M. A. photo Theban Tomb 1874. My thanks to Dorothea Arnold and Marsha Hill for access to this photograph. This description should also serve as a correction of statements misidentifying this scene in E. Bleiberg, "Kings," 164n.30.

60. *Urk.* IV, 326:2–3.

61. Ibid., 512:5–6.

62. Ibid., 523:5–6.

63. Ibid., 930:11.

64. J. Yoyotte, "Le général Thouti et la perception des tributs syriens," *BSFE* 92 (1981): 33–51.

65. *Urk.* IV, 1094:6–1095:3.

66. Ibid., 1097:7–16; see also 1099:4–5, 1100:6–7, 1102:5–6.

67. N. de G. Davies, *The Tomb of Rekhmire* (New York, 1944), pl. xlix.

68. *KRI* III, 9:5 ff.

69. *Urk.* IV, 1115:12.

70. Ibid., 1114:3.

71. *Wb.* III, 251.

72. P. Smither, "A Tax Assessor's Journal of the Middle Kingdom," *JEA* 27 (1941): 75.

73. M. de Rochemonteix and E. Chassinat, *Temple,* vol. 1, (1897), 188; vol. 2, 40, 50. See P. Smither, "Tax," 75.

74. *Urk.* IV, 1397:15–1380:3.

75. J. Černý, *Coptic Etymological Dictionary* (Cambridge, 1976), 237.

76. *Wb.* III, 253.

77. *Urk.* IV, 1380:1.

78. P. Virey, "Le tombeau d'Am-n-t'eh et la fonction de *imy-r rwyt,*" *RT* 7 (1886), 32.

79. *Urk.* IV, 523:15–524:2.

Chapter Five

1. See remarks in D. Müller, "Neue Urkunden zur Verwaltung in Mittleren Reich," *Orientalia,* n.s. 36 (1967): 351.

2. W. Helck, "Die 'Weihinschrift' aus dem Taltempel des Sonnenheiligtums des Königs Neusserre bei Abu Gurob," *SAK* 5 (1977): 57. On festival dates in general, see A. Spalinger, "A Chronological Analysis of the Festival of *ṯḫy,*" *SAK* 20 (1993): 289–304.

3. W. Decker, *Sports,* 72 ff.

4. H. H. Nelson et al., vol. 2, pl. 3.

5. G. Fourcart, *Tombes thébaines. Nécropole de Dira Abu'-n-Naga. Le*

tombeau d'Amonmos IV (Cairo, 1935), pl. 13.

6. W. Decker, *Sports,* 81–82.

7. Ibid., *Sports,* 81.

8. N. de G. Davies, *Rock Tombs,* vol. 2, pl. 37.

9. N. de G. Davies, *The Tomb of Rekhmire at Thebes,* vol. 1 (New York, 1944), 15.

10. N. de G. Davies, *The Tomb of Puyemre at Thebes* (New York, 1922–23), pls. 35–39.; N. de G. Davies, *The Tomb of Rekhmire at Thebes,* vol. 1, 15.

Bibliography

Aldred, C. "The Foreign Gifts Offered to Pharaoh." *JEA* 56 (1970): 105–16.
——. "Year Twelve at el-Amarna." *JEA* 43 (1957): 114–17.
Allam, S. "Silber = Leistung (in Form von beweglichen Vermögensgegenstände)." *Orientalia,* n.s. 36 (1967): 416–20.
Altenmüller, H., and A. Moussa. "Die Inschrift Amenemhets II aus den Ptahtempel von Memphis: Ein Vorbericht." *SAK* 18 (1991): 1–48, and *Falttafel* 1.
Amélineau, E. *Les nouvelles Fouilles d'Abydos.* 3 vols. Angers: A. Burdin, 1896–98.
Arnold, Dor. "Amenemhat I and the Early Twelfth Dynasty at Thebes." *MMJ* 26 (1991): 5–48.
Ayrton, E. R. *Abydos.* 3 vols. Memoirs of the Egypt Exploration Society 22–24. London: Egypt Exploration Society, 1902–1904.
Baer, K. "An Eleventh Dynasty Farmer's Letters." *JAOS* 83 (1963): 1–19.
——. "The Low Price of Land in Ancient Egypt." *JARCE* 1 (1962): 25–45.
Baines, J. *Fecundity Figures: Egyptian Personification and the Iconology of a Genre.* Chicago: Bolchazy-Carducci, 1985.
Bakir, A. M. *Slavery in Pharaonic Egypt.* Cairo: IFAO, 1952.

Bénédite, G. "The Carnarvon Ivory." *JEA* 5 (1918): 1–15.
Bissing, Fr. W. v. "Miscellen." *ZÄS* 40 (1902): 95–98.
Blackman, A. *Middle Egyptian Stories.* Bibliotheca Aegyptiaca 2. Bruxelles: Éditions de la Fondation égyptologique reine Élisabeth, 1932.
——. *The Rock Tombs of Meir.* 6 vols. ASE 22–25, 28–29. London: Egypt Exploration Society, 1914–53.
——. "The Stele of Thethi, Brit. Mus. No. 614," *JEA* 17 (1931): 55–61.
Blackman, A., and T. E. Peet, "Papyrus Lansing: A Translation with Notes." *JEA* 11 (1925): 284–98.
Bleiberg, E. "Aspects of the Political, Religious, and Economic Basis of Egyptian Imperialism during the New Kingdom." Unpublished Ph.D. dissertation, University of Toronto, 1984.
——. "Commodity Exchange in the Annals of Thutmose III." *JSSEA* 11 (1981): 107–10.
——. "The King's Privy Purse during the New Kingdom: An Examination of *INW.*" *JARCE* 21 (1984): 155–67.
——. "The Redistributive Economy in New Kingdom Egypt: An Examination of *B3KW(T).*" *JARCE* 25 (1988): 157–68.
Blumenthal, E. *Untersuchungen zum Ägyptischen Königtum des Mittleren Reiches,* vol. 1. Berlin: Akademie Verlag, 1970.
Borchardt, L. *Denkmäler des Alten Reiches (ausser Statuen) im Museum von Kairo, nr. 1295–1808.* Berlin: Reichsdruckerei, 1937.
——. "Ein Rechnungsbuch des königlichen Hofes aus dem Ende des Mittleren Reiches." *ZÄS* 28 (1890): 65–103.
Brack, A. *Das Grab des Tjanuni.* Mainz: Verlag Phillip von Zabern, 1977.
Breasted, J. *Ancient Records of Egypt.* Chicago: University of Chicago Press, 1906–1907.
Brunner, H. *Die Lehre des Cheti, Sohnes des Duauf.* Ägyptologische Forschungen, 13. Glückstadt and Hamburg: Verlag J. J. Augustin, 1944.
——. *Die Texte aus den Gräbern der Herakleopolitenzeit von Siut.* Ägyptologische Forschungen 5. Glückstadt: J.J. Augustin, 1937.
Budge, E. A. W. *An Egyptian Hieroglyphic Dictionary.* London: J. Murray, 1920.
Caminos, R. A. *Late Egyptian Miscellanies.* London: Oxford University Press, 1954.
——. *Literary Fragments in the Hieratic Script.* Oxford: Griffith Institute, 1956.

Capart, J. "Note sur un fragment de bas-relief au British Museum." *BIFAO* 30 (1931): 73–75.
Castle, E. "Shipping and Trade in Ramesside Egypt." *JESHO* 35 (1992): 206–38.
Černý, J. *Coptic Etymological Dictionary.* Cambridge: Cambridge University Press, 1976.
——. "Prices and Wages in Egypt in the Ramesside Period." *Cahiers d'histoire mondiale* 1 (1951): 903–21.
Couyat, J., and P. Montet. *Les inscriptions hiéroglyphiques et hiératique du Ouâdi Hammâmât.* MIFAO 34. Cairo: IFAO, 1912–13.
Crum, W. *A Coptic Dictionary.* Oxford: Clarendon Press, 1929–39.
Curtis, J. W. "Coinage in Pharaonic Egypt." *JEA* 43 (1957): 71–77.
Dalton, G. *Economic Anthropology and Development.* New York: Natural History Press, 1971.
——., ed., *Primitive and Modern Economics: Essays of Karl Polanyi.* Boston: Beacon Press, 1971.
Davies, N. de G. *The Mastabah of Ptahhetep and Akhethetep at Saqqara.* 2 vols. ASE 8,9. London: Egypt Exploration Fund, 1900–1901.
——. *Rock Tombs of El Amarna.* 5 vols. London: Kegan Paul, Trench, Trübner, and Co., 1903–1908.
——. *The Tomb of Puyemre at Thebes.* New York: Metropolitan Museum of Art, 1922–23.
——. *The Tomb of Rekhmire at Thebes.* 2 vols. New York: Metropolitan Museum of Art, 1944.
Decker, W. "Neue Dokumente zum Ringkampf in alten Ägypten." *Kölner Beiträge zur Sportwissenschaft* 5 (1976): 7–24.
——. "Ringen." *LdÄ* 5 (1984): 265–66.
——. *Sports and Games of Ancient Egypt.* New Haven: Yale University Press, 1992.
Dziobek, E. *Das Grab des Ineni: Theben Nr. 81.* Mainz: Verlag Phillip von Zabern, 1992.
Edel, E. "Inschriften des Alten Reiches. V. Die Reisebericht des *Ḥrw- ḫwjf* (Her-chuf)." In *Ägyptologische Studien,* edited by O. Firchow, 51–75. Berlin: Akademie Verlag, 1955.
Emery, W. *Great Tombs of the First Dynasty.* Vol. 1, Excavations at Saqqara 1937–38. Cairo: Government Press, 1949.
——. *Great Tombs of the First Dynasty.* Vol. 2, Memoirs of the Egypt Exploration Society, 46. London: Oxford University Press, 1954.
——. *Great Tombs of the First Dynasty.* Vol. 3, Memoirs of the Egypt Exploration Society, 47. London: Egypt Exploration Society,

1958
——. *The Tomb of Hemaka.* Excavations at Saqqara, n.d. Cairo: Government Press, 1938
——. *The Tomb of Hor-Aha.* Excavations at Saqqara 1937–38. Cairo: Government Press, 1939.
Erichsen, W. *Demotisches Glossar.* Copenhagen: E. Mundgaard, 1954.
——. *Papyrus Harris I.* Bibliotheca Aegyptiaca 5. Bruxelles: Éditions de la Fondation égyptologique reine Élisabeth, 1933.
Erman, A., and H. Grapow. *Wörterbuch der Ägyptische Sprache.* Leipzig: J. C. Hindrichs'sche Buchhandlung, 1926–50.
——. *Reden Rufe u. Lieder auf Gräberbildern des Alten Reiches.* Berlin: Akademie der Wissenschaften, 1919.
Eyre, C. "An Accounts Papyrus from Thebes," *JEA* 66 (1980): 108–19.
——. "Work and Organization of Work in the Old Kingdom." In *Labor in the Ancient Near East,* edited by M. A. Powell, 5–47. New Haven: American Oriental Society, 1987.
Faulkner, R. O. *Concise Dictionary of Middle Egyptian.* Oxford: Griffith Institute, 1962.
——. "The Wars of Sethos I." *JEA* 33 (1947): 34–39.
Firth, R. *Themes in Economic Anthropology.* Association of Social Anthropologists Monograph 6. London: Tavistock, 1967.
Fischer, H. "The Nubian Mercenaries of Gebelein during the First Intermediate Period." *Kush* 9 (1961): 44–80.
——. "Old Kingdom Inscriptions in the Yale Gallery." *Mitteilungen des Instituts für Orientforschung* 7 (1960): 299–315.
Forde, D., and M. Douglas, "Primitive Economics." In *Tribal and Peasant Economies,* edited by G. Dalton, 23–28. Garden City, N.Y.: Natural History Press, 1967.
Fourcart, G. *Tombes thébaines. Nécropole de Dira Abu'-n-Naga. Le tombeau d'Amonmos IV.* MMMAFC 57. Cairo: IFAO, 1935.
Franke, D. "The Career of Khnumhotep III of Beni Hasan and the So-called 'Decline of the Nomarchs.' " In *Middle Kingdom Studies,* edited by S. Quirke, 51–68. New Malden: Sia Publishing, 1991.
Frankfort, H., and J. D. S. Pendlebury, *The City of Akhenaten,* Part 2. Egypt Exploration Society Memoirs 40. London: Egypt Exploration Society, 1933.
Gamer-Wallert, I. *Fische und Fischkulte im Alten Ägypten.* Ägyptologische Abhandlungen 21. Wiesbaden: Harrassowitz, 1970.
Gardiner, A. *The Admonitions of an Egyptian Sage.* Hildesheim: Georg Olms Verlag, 1969.

——. *Ancient Egyptian Onomastica.* London: Oxford University Press, 1947.
——. *Egyptian Grammar.* Oxford: Griffith Institute, 1957.
——. "Inscriptions from the Tomb of Si-renpowet I, Prince of Elephantine." *ZÄS* 45 (1908): 123–40.
——. *Late Egyptian Miscellanies.* Bibliotheca Aegyptiaca 7. Bruxelles: Éditions de la Fondation égyptologique reine Élisabeth, 1937.
——. *Late Egyptian Stories.* Bibliotheca Aegyptiaca 1. Bruxelles: Éditions de la Fondation égyptologique reine Élisabeth, 1932.
——. "A Lawsuit Arising from the Purchase of Two Slaves," *JEA* 21 (1935): 140–46.
——. "A Pharaonic Encomium." *JEA* 41 (1955): 30 and pls. VII–XI.
——. "Ramesside Texts Relating to the Taxation and Transport of Corn." *JEA* 27 (1941): 19–73.
Garstang, J. "The Tablet of Mena." *ZÄS* 42 (1905): 61–75.
Gauthier, H. "La Grande Inscription dédicatoire d'Abydos." *ZÄS* 48 (1911): 52–66.
——. *La Grande Inscription dédicatoire d'Abydos.* BdÉ 4. Cairo: IFAO, 1912.
Gayet, A. J. *Musée du Louvre Stèles de la XIIe dynastie.* Paris: F. Vieweg, 1889.
Georgescu-Roegen, N. *Analytical Economics: Issues and Problems.* Cambridge: Harvard University Press, 1966.
Gestermann, L. *Kontinuität und Wandel in Politik und Verwaltung des Früh Mittleren Reiches in Ägypten.* Wiesbaden: Harrassowitz, 1987.
Glanville, S. "Records of a Dockyard of the Time of Thutmosis III: Papyrus British Museum 10,056." *ZÄS* 66 (1931): 105–21. Reprinted in *ZÄS* 68 (1932): 7–41.
Goedicke, H. "Abi-Sha(i)'s Representation in Beni Hasan." *JARCE* 21 (1984): 203–10.
——. *Studies in the Hekanakhte Papers.* Baltimore: Helgo Press, 1984.
Gordon, A. "The Context and Meaning of the Ancient Egyptian Word INW from the Proto-Dynastic Period to the End of the New Kingdom." Unpublished Ph.D. dissertation, University of California, Berkeley, 1985.
Grapow, H. *Studien zu den Annalen Thutmosis des dritten . . .* APAW 1947. Berlin: Akademie Verlag, 1947.
Grdseloff, B. "Notes sur deux Monuments inédits de l'Ancien Empire." *ASAE* 42 (1943): 107–25.
Grierson, P. "The Origins of Money." *Research in Economic Anthropology*

1 (1978): 1–36.
Griffith, F. L. "The Abydos Decree of Seti I at Nauri." *JEA* 13 (1927): 193–208.
——. "The Account Papyrus No. 18 of Boulaq." *ZÄS* 29 (1891): 102–16.
——. *The Petrie Papyri: Hieratic Papyri from Kahun and Gurob.* London: B. Quaritich, 1898.
Guglielmi, W. "Die Feldgöttin *sḫ.t.*" *Die Welt des Orients* 7 (1974): 206–27.
——. "Sechat." *LdÄ* 5 (1984): 778.
Guksch, H. *Das Grab des Benja, gen. Paheqamen: Theben Nr 343.* Mainz: Verlag Phillip von Zabern, 1978.
Gunn, B. "Inscriptions of 1922." In *City of Akhenaten,* vol. 1, edited by T. E. Peet and C. L. Wooley. Memoirs of the Egypt Exploration Society 38. London: Egypt Exploration Society, 1923.
Halperin, R. "The Concept of the Formal in Economic Anthropology." *Research in Economic Anthropology* 7 (1985): 339–68.
——. "Polanyi, Marx, and the Institutional Paradigm in Economic Anthropology." *Research in Economic Anthropology* 6 (1984): 245–72.
Harpur, Y. *Decoration in Egyptian Tombs of the Old Kingdom.* London: Kegan Paul, 1987.
Hassan, S. *Excavations at Giza.* 10 vols. Cairo: Government Press, 1929–60.
Hayes, W. C. "Inscriptions from the Palace of Amenhotep III." *JNES* 10 (1951): 32, 82, 156, 231.
——. "Notes on the Government of Egypt in the Late Middle Kingdom." *JNES* 12 (1953): 31–39.
Helck, W. *Die Beziehungen Ägyptens zu Vorderasian im 3. und 2. Jahrtausend v. Chr.* (2. verbesserte Auflage). Ägyptologische Abhandlungen 5. Wiesbaden: Harrassowitz, 1971.
——. *Geschichte des Alten Ägypten.* Leiden: Brill, 1968.
——. *Die Lehre des Dw3-ḫtjj.* Wiesbaden: Harrassowitz, 1970.
——. *Die Lehre für König Merikare.* Wiesbaden: Harrassowitz, 1977.
——. "Naqada." *LdÄ* 4 (1980): 344–46.
——. "Thothfest." *LdÄ* 6 (1985): 523.
——. *Urkunden der 18. Dynastie.* Leipzig: Akademie Verlag, 1956–58.
——. *Urkunden der 18. Dynastie: Übersetzung zu den Heften 17–22.* Berlin: Akademie Verlag, 1961.
——. *Untersuchungen zur Thinitenzeit.* Wiesbaden: Harrassowitz, 1989.

——. "Die 'Weihinschrift' aus dem Taltempel des Sonnenheiligtums des Königs Neusserre bei Abu Gurob." *SAK* 5 (1977): 47–77.

——. *Wirtschaftsgeschichte des alten Ägypten in 3. und 2. Jahrtausend v. Chr.* Leiden: Brill, 1975.

Herskovits, M. *Economic Anthropology.* New York: Knopf, 1952.

Hoffman, M. *Egypt Before the Pharaohs.* Rev. ed. Austin: University of Texas Press, 1991.

Hölzl, C. "Studien zur Entwicklung der Felsengräber: Datierung und lockale Entwicklung der Felsengräber des Mittleren Reiches in Mittelägypten." Unpublished Ph.D. dissertation, University of Vienna, n.d.

Jacquet-Gordon, H. *Les Noms des Domaines funéraires sous l'Ancien Empire égyptien.* BdÉ 34. Cairo: IFAO, 1962.

James, T. G. H. *The Hekanakhte Papers and Other Early Middle Kingdom Documents.* Egyptian Expedition Publications 19. New York: Metropolitan Museum of Art, 1962.

Janssen, J. J. "*b3kw*: From Work to Product." *SAK* 20 (1993): 81–94.

——. *Commodity Prices from the Ramessid Period.* Leiden: Brill, 1975.

——. "Economic History during the New Kingdom." *SAK* 3 (1975): 127–86.

——. "Gift Giving in Ancient Egypt as an Economic Feature." *JEA* 68 (1982): 253–58.

Jeffreys, D., and J. Málek. "Memphis 1984." *JEA* 72 (1986): 1–14.

——. "Memphis 1986, 1987." *JEA* 74 (1988): 15–30.

Junker, H. *Bericht über die Grabungen . . . auf dem Friedhof in Turah.* Denkschrift der Kaiserlichen Akademie der Wissenschaften in Wien 56. Vienna: Alfred Holder, 1912.

——. *Giza.* 12 vols. Vienna: Hölder-Pickler-Tempsky, 1929–44.

Kahl, J. *Das System der Ägyptischen Hieroglyphenschrift in der 0–3 Dynastie.* Wiesbaden: Harrassowitz, 1994.

Kaiser, W. *Ägyptisches Museum Berlin.* Berlin: Brüder Hartmann, 1967.

Kaplony, P. *Beschriftete Kleinfunde in der Sammlung Georges Michaelidis.* Uitgaven van het Nederlands Historisch-Archaeologisch Instituut te Istanbul 32. Istanbul: Nederlands Historisch-Archaeologisch Instituut in Het Nabije Oosten, 1973.

——. *Die Inschriften der ägyptischer Frühzeit.* 3 vols. Ägyptologische Abhandlungen 8. Wiesbaden: Harrassowitz, 1963.

——. *Steingefässe mit Inschriften der Frühzeit und des Alten Reiches.* Monumenta Aegyptiaca 1. Bruxelles: Editons de la Fondation égyptologique reine Élisabeth, 1968.

Kaplony-Heckel, U. *Ägyptische Handschriften.* Verzeichnis der Orientalischen Handschriften in Deutschland XIX, 1. Wiesbaden: Franz Steiner Verlag, 1971.

Kees, H. "Zur Bedeutung vom *wᶜrt* in Urkunden der M.R." *ZÄS* 70 (1934): 86–91.

Kemp, B. "Abydos and the Royal Tombs of the First Dynasty." *JEA* 52 (1966): 13–22.

——. *Ancient Egypt: Anatomy of a Civilization.* London: Routledge, 1989.

——. "Imperialism and Empire in New Kingdom Egypt." In *Imperialism in the Ancient World,* edited by P. D. A. Garnsey and C. R. Whittaker, 7–57. Cambridge: Cambridge University Faculty of Classics, 1978.

Kessler, D. "Die Asiatenkarawane von Beni Hassan." *SAK* 14 (1987): 147–65.

Kitchen, K. *Ramesside Inscriptions.* 8 vols. Oxford: Blackwell, 1975–90.

Lacau, P., and J-Ph. Lauer. *La Pyramide à degrés.* 5 vols. Cairo: IFAO, 1936–65.

Leahy, M. A. *Excavations at Malkatta: The Inscriptions.* Warminster: Aris and Philips, 1978.

Leprohon, R. J. "Some Remarks on the 'Administrative Department' (*wᶜrt*) of the Late Middle Kingdom." *JSSEA* 10 (1980): 163–64.

Lepsius, C. R. *Denkmäler aus Ägypten und Äthiopien.* 12 vols. Berlin: Nicolai, 1849–59.

Lichtheim, M. *Ancient Egyptian Literature.* 3 vols. Berkeley: University of California Press, 1976.

Liverani, M. "Memorandum on the Approach to Historiographic Texts." *Orientalia,* n.s. 42 (1973): 178–94.

Lorton, D. *The Juridical Terminology of International Relations in Egyptian Texts through Dyn. XVIII.* Baltimore: Johns Hopkins University Press, 1974.

——. "The So-called 'Vile' Enemies of the King of Egypt (in the Middle Kingdom and Dynasty XVIII)." *JARCE* 10 (1973): 71–76.

Macramallah, R. *Un cimetière archaïque de la classe moyenne du peuple à Saqqarah.* Cairo: Imprimerie National, 1940.

Mariette, A. *Les Mastabas de l'Ancien Empire.* Hildesheim and New York: Georg Olms Verlag, 1976.

Martin, G. *Memphite Tomb of Horemheb, Commander in Chief of Tutankhamun.* Egypt Exploration Society Memoirs 55. London: Egypt Exploration Society, 1989.

Mauss, M. *The Gift.* London: Cohen and West, 1954.

Meeks, D. *Année Lexicographique.* Paris: Inprimerie de la Margaride, 1980.

Megally, M. *Le Papyrus hiératique comptable E. 3226 du Louvre.* Cairo: IFAO, 1971.

Montet, P. *Les reliques de l'art syrien dans l'Égypte du Nouvel Empire.* Paris: Les Belles Lettres, 1937.

Müller, D. "Neue Urkunden zur Verwaltung im Mittleren Reich." *Orientalia,* n.s., 36 (1967): 351–64.

Müller-Wollermann, R. "Bemerkungen zu den sogenannten Tributen." *GM* 66 (1983): 81–94.

——. "Waren Austausch im Ägypten des Alten Reiches." *JESHO* 28 (1985): 121–68.

Munn-Rankin, J. M. "Diplomacy in Western Asia in the Early Second Millennium, B.C." *Iraq* 18 (1956): 68–110.

Naville, E. *Cemeteries of Abydos,* vol. 1. Memoirs of the Egypt Exploration Fund 33. London: Egypt Exploration Fund, 1914.

Nelson, H. H. et al. *Later Historical Records of Rameses III: Medinet Habu II.* Oriental Institute Publications 9. Chicago: Oriental Institute, 1932.

Newberry, P. *Beni Hasan.* 4 vols. London: Egypt Exploration Fund, 1893–1919.

——. *El Bersheh.* 2 vols. London: Egypt Exploration Fund, 1893–94.

North, D. "Government and the Cost of Exchange in History." *Journal of Economic History* 44 (1984): 255–64.

——. "Markets and Other Allocation Systems in History: The Challenge of Karl Polanyi." *Journal of European Economic History* 6 (1977): 703–16.

Northhampton, Marquis of, W. Spiegelberg, and P. E. Newberry. *Report on Some Excavations in the Theban Necropolis.* London: Constable, 1908.

Paget, R. F. E., and A. A. Pirie, *The Tomb of Ptahhetep.* London: Histories and Mysteries of Man, 1989.

Parkinson, R. B. *The Tale of the Eloquent Peasant.* Oxford: Griffith Institute, 1991.

Peet, T. E. "The Egyptian Words for 'Money,' 'Buy,' and 'Sell,' In *Studies Presented to F. Ll. Griffith,* edited by S. R. K. Glanville, 122–27. London: Egypt Exploration Society, 1932.

——. *The Great Tomb-Robberies of the Twentieth Egyptian Dynasty.* Oxford: Clarendon Press, 1930.

Petrie, W. M. F. *Royal Tombs of the Earliest Dynasties.* Vol. 2. Memoirs of the Egypt Exploration Fund 21. London: Egypt Exploration Fund, 1901.

Pierret, P. *Recueil d'inscriptions inédites du Musée égyptien du Louvre.* Paris: A. Franck, 1874–78.

Polanyi, K. *The Livelihood of Man.* New York: Academic Press, 1977.

Porter, B., and R. Moss. *Topographical Bibliography of Ancient Egyptian Hieroglyphic Texts, Reliefs, and Paintings.* 2nd rev. ed. edited by J. Málek. Oxford: Griffith Institute, 1974–present.

Posener, G. "A New Inscription of the XIIth Dynasty." *JSSEA* 12 (1982): 7–8.

Posener-Kriéger, P. *Les archives du temple funéraire de Néferirkarê-Kakaï (Les papyrus d'Abousir).* 2 vols. BdÉ 65. Cairo: IFAO, 1976.

Posener-Kriéger, P., and J. L. de Cénival, eds. *Hieratic Papyri in the British Museum: The Abu-Sir Papyri.* London: British Museum, 1968.

Pritchard, J. *Ancient Near Eastern Texts Relating to the Old Testament.* Princeton: Princeton University Press, 1969.

Quirke, S. *The Administration of Egypt in the Late Middle Kingdom: The Hieratic Documents.* New Malden: Sia Press, 1990.

Ratié, S. *La reine Hatchepsout: Sources et problèmes.* Leiden: Brill, 1979.

Redford, D. B. *History and Chronology of the Eighteenth Dynasty: Seven Studies.* Toronto: University of Toronto Press, 1967.

Reinecke, W. "Waren die *šwtyw* wirklich Kaufleute?" *AoF* 6 (1979): 5–14.

Renger, J. "Patterns of Non-Institutional Trade and Non-Commercial Exchange in Ancient Mesopotamia." In *Circulation of Goods in Non-Palatial Context in the Ancient Near East,* edited by A. Archi, 31–124 Rome: Edizioni dell'Ateneo, 1984.

Rochemonteix, M. de, and E. Chassinat. *Le Temple d'Edfou.* MMMAFC 10. Cairo: MMAFC, 1897.

Roth, A. *Egyptian Phyles in the Old Kingdom: The Evolution of a System of Social Organization.* SAOC 48. Chicago: University of Chicago Press, 1991.

Säve-Söderbergh, T. *The Navy of the Eighteenth Dynasty.* Uppsala: Ludequistka, 1946.

Scharff, A. *Die Altertümer der Vor- und Frühzeit Ägyptens.* 2 vols. Berlin: K. Curtius, 1931.

——. *Archäologische Beiträge zur Frage der Entstehung der Hieroglyphenschrift.* Hildesheim: Gerstenberg, 1975.

——. "Ein Rechnungsbuch des Königlichen Hofes aus der 13. Dynastie." *ZÄS* 57 (1922): 51–68 and 1**-24**.

Schenkel, W. *Frühmittelägyptische Studien.* Bonner Orientalische Studien, n.s. 13. Bonn: Orientalischen Seminars der Universität Bonn, 1962.

——. *Memphis, Herakleopolis, Theben.* Ägyptologische Abhandlungen 12. Wiesbaden: Harrassowitz, 1965.

Schott, S. "Hieroglyphen: Untersuchungen zum Ursprung der Schrift." *Akademie der Wissenschaften und Literatur. Abhandlungen der Geistes- und Sozialwissenschaftlichen Klasse,* Jahrg. 1950, No. 24.

Schulman, A. "Diplomatic Marriage in the Egyptian New Kingdom." *JNES* (1973): 177–93.

Sethe, K. *Die Altägyptischen Pyramidentexte.* 4 vols. Leipzig: J. C. Hindrichs'sche Buchhandlung, 1908–22.

——. *Urkunden der 18. Dynastie.* Leipzig: Akademie Verlag, 1906–1909.

——. *Urkunden des Alten Reiches.* Leipzig: J. C. Hindrichs'sche Buchhandlung, 1909.

Sethe, K., and W. Erichsen. *Historisch-biographische Urkunden des Mittleren Reiches.* Leipzig: J. C. Hindrichs'sche Buchhandlung, 1935.

Seyfried, K-J. *Beiträge zu den Expeditionen des Mittleren Reiches in die Ost-Wüste.* HÄB 15. Hildesheim: Pelizaeus Museum, 1981.

Shorter, A. "Historical Scarabs of Thuthmosis IV and Amenophis III." *JEA* 17 (1931): 23–25.

Silver, M. *Economic Structures of the Ancient Near East.* Totowa, N.J.: Barnes and Noble, 1985.

Simpson, W. K. *Hekanefer and the Dynastic Material from Toshka and Arminna.* Publications of the Pennsylvania-Yale Expedition to Egypt 1. New Haven and Philadelphia: Peabody Museum of Natural History, 1963.

——., ed. *The Literature of Ancient Egypt.* New Haven: Yale University Press, 1973.

——. *Papyrus Reisner.* 4 vols. Boston: Museum of Fine Arts, 1963–84.

Smith, H. S. "Walter Bryan Emery." *JEA* 57 (1971): 199.

Smithers, P. "A Tax Assessor's Journal of the Middle Kingdom." *JEA* 27 (1941): 74–76.

Spalinger, A. "A Chronological Analysis of the Festival of *ṯḫy.*" *SAK* 20 (1993): 289–304.

——. "A Critical Analysis of the 'Annals' of Thutmose III." *JARCE* 14 (1977): 41–54.

——. "Foods in P. Boulaq 18." *SAK* 13 (1986): 207–48.

——. "Notes on the Day Summary Accounts of P. Boulaq 18 and Intradepartmental Transfers." *SAK* 12 (1985): 179–242.
——. "Some Revisions of Temple Endowments in the New Kingdom." *JARCE* 28 (1991): 21–40.
Spanel, D. "Beni Hasan in the Herakleopolitan Period." Unpublished Ph.D. dissertation, University of Toronto, 1984.
Spencer, A. J. *Early Egypt: The Rise of Civilization in the Nile Valley.* London: British Museum, 1993.
Touney, A. D., and S. Wenig. *Der Sport im Alten Ägypten.* Leipzig: Edition Leipzig, 1969.
Vandier, J. *Manuel d'archéologie égyptienne.* 5 vols. Paris: Éditions A. et J. Picard, 1952.
——. *Mo'alla: La tombe d' Ankhtifi et la tombe de Sebekhotep.* BdÉ, 18. Cairo: IFAO, 1950.
Vikentiev, V. "Études d'épigraphie protodynastique." *ASAE* 56 (1959): 3–30.
——. "Les Monuments archaïques VI." *BIÉ* 36 (1954): 293–315.
——. "Les Monuments archaïques IV–V." *BIÉ* 32 (1951): 171–223.
Virey, P. "Le tombeau d'Am-n-t'eh et la fonction de *imy-r rwyt.*" *Recueil de Travaux* 7 (1886): 32–46.
Vogelsang, F. *Kommentar zu den Klagen des Bauern.* Untersuchungen zur Geschichte und Altertumskunde Ägypten 6. Leipzig: J. C. Hindrichs'sche Buchhandlung, 1913.
Volten, A. *Zwei altägyptische politische Schriften: Die Lehre für König Merikare (Pap. Carlsberg VI) und die Lehre des Königs Amenemhet.* Copenhagen: E. Munksgaard, 1945.
Ward, W. *Index of Egyptian Administrative and Religious Titles of the Middle Kingdom.* Beirut: American University of Beirut Press, 1982.
Willems, H. O. "The Nomarchs of the Hare Nome and Early Middle Kingdom History." *JEOL* 28 (1985): 80–102.
Yoyotte, J. "Le général Thouti et la perception des tributs syriens." *BSFE* 92 (1981): 33–51.
Zaccagnini, C. *Lo scambio dei doni nel vicino oriente durante i secoli xv–xiii.* Orientis antiqui collectio 11. Rome: Centro per le Antichità e la Storia del'Arte del Vicino Oriente, 1973.
Zivie, C. *Giza au deuxième millénaire.* BdÉ 70. Cairo: IFAO, 1976.

Index of Egyptian Sources

Papyri

Abu Sir Papyri, 43, 45–48, 52, 53, 117, 118, 123

Berlin papyri, 74, 82

Gardiner archives, 145n.42

Hekanakht, archive of, 20

Illahun papyri, 118, 123

Papyri, miscellaneous, 115–16, 120; of Kahun, 84; royal account, 74–78, 84–85
Papyrus Amiens, 17, 18
Papyrus Anastasi, 17–18
Papyrus B.M., 19, 23
Papyrus Boulaq, 74, 76, 85, 88, 100, 118, 123
Papyrus Harageh, 112
Papyrus Koller, 106, 121
Papyrus Lansing, 12–14, 18
Papyrus Louvre, 16–17. See also *Papyrus Amiens*
Papyrus Sallier, 15
Papyrus Turin, 103, 105–106, 118
Petrie papyri, 74

Report of Wenamun, 18–19, 25

Tomb Robbery Papyri, 18, 22

Wilbour Papyrus, 146n.53

Inscriptions and Other Documents

Annals, royal, 57–58, 93, 95, 97
Annals of Amenemhet II, 71, 122

Annals of Thutmose III, 4–5
Archives, mortuary temple, 74, 76, 88, 116, 145n.42
Autobiographies, tomb, 67, 70

Berlin Stele, 12, 13, 17
Biographies, tomb, 20, 24, 44–46, 55, 64–65, 111–13, 118, 119. *See also* Autobiographies, tomb

Captions, tomb-scene, 101, 104, 106, 109, 110, 113, 115, 121
Columns, inscribed, 94

Dockets, jar, 100
Documents, government, 116
Duties of the Vizier, The, 108, 112

Edict of Horemheb, 17

Inscriptions, 44, 57, 65, 98, 104, 115, 116; architrave, 94; jar, 29, 37; royal, 93, 115, 116; statuary, 109; temple, 102; Theban, 54. *See also* Annals, royal; Columns, inscribed; Monuments, inscribed; Scarab, inscribed

Jars. *See* Dockets, jar; Inscriptions, jar; Labels, jar

Labels, jar, 29–30, 35, 38, 41, 42, 51, 52, 115, 116, 118
Letters, 99, 105
Lists, donor, 101, 102
Literature, Egyptian, 86–88, 115, 116. See also *Duties of the Vizier, The*
Louvre Stela, 16

Monuments, inscribed, 90, 124

Nauri Decree, 14–15

Palermo Stone, 43, 45, 52

Records, temple, 77–83
Reliefs, wall, 21, 93, 102, 109, 118, 121; captions to, 101

Scarab, inscribed, 94
Scenes, tomb. *See* Walls, tomb/temple
Seals, jar. *See* Labels, jar
Sphinx Stela, 91
Statues. *See* Inscriptions, statuary; Monuments
Stelae, 91, 92
Stela of Hor-meni, 92

Tags. *See* Labels
Tjetjy Stele, 57

Wadi Hammamat Inscription, 24
Walls, tomb/temple, 43, 47–52, 58–63, 66–73, 88, 101, 104–10, 120, 142n.1. *See also* Biographies, tomb; Inscriptions; Reliefs, wall
Wisdom text, 55

General Index

Aakheperkare. *See* Thutmose I
Abydos, Eg., 32, 35–37
Admonitions of an Egyptian Sage, 86, 87
Aha (king), 34
Akhenaton (king), 121
Akhethotep (official), 48, 51, 53, 72
Aldred, Cyril, 105–106
Alexander the Great, 25
Amarna, Eg., 21–22, 120, 121
Amarna Letters, 99
Amarna Period, 122
Amélineau, Émile C., 32
Amenemhet (nomarch), 64–67, 69
Amenemhet I, 24, 59, 60, 143n.13
Amenemhet II, 57–58, 63, 65, 67, 70, 71, 73, 88, 122. *See also* Annals of Amenemhet II *in Index of Egyptian Sources*
Amenemhet III, 74, 76–84
Amenhotep (scribe), 98
Amenhotep (son of Hapu), 99
Amenhotep II, 58, 94
Amenhotep III, 42, 94, 99–101
Amenmesse, 121
Amen-Re (god), 25
Amun (god), 17–18, 24, 92, 99, 102
Amun-Re (god), 102
Animals: as *inw*, 47, 49, 50, 59, 62–63, 66, 68, 70, 71, 74, 75, 100, 101, 104, 108, 113, 122; taxes on, 67; trade in, 12, 26. *See also* Hides; Hunting
Ankhtyfy, 20
Antef (official), 122
Anubis (god), 77, 82, 88

Archaic Period, *inw* during, 29–42, 87, 88, 115, 117–20
Asia, *inw* from, 95, 109, 111
Assyria, Egypt and, 99
Aswan, Eg., 44–45, 64, 116

Babylonia, Egypt and, 99
Baqet I, 59–63, 68–71, 73, 108, 119, 121
Baqet II, 62, 69, 121
Baqet III, 66, 68, 69, 143n.13
Barter, 9, 16, 21, 23, 24, 26
Bat emblem, 142n.1
Bee (symbol), 30, 36
Beni Hasan, Eg., 58, 119; tombs at, 59, 60, 62, 64, 66–70, 88, 108, 143nn.13,15
Benya-Pahekamen (overseer), 108
Bersheh, Eg., 58, 65, 68, 70, 88
Boats, Egyptian, 12–15, 17–18, 135n.63
Brunner, H., 15–16, 134n.44
B3kw(t), 4–5
Bty (term), 15–16, 134n.44
Bulti-fish (symbol), 30
Byblos, Phoe., 111

Capitalism, 5, 8
Caravans, 70
Chapels, tomb, 49
Children, in tomb illustrations, 50, 51, 60
Cloth, trade in, 20, 26
Coinage, and money contrasted, 25
Copper, 16, 25, 26
Coronations, 105–106
Curds, 100

Dates (fruit), 16–17
De(we)n (king), 34, 48
Djheutyhotep II, 65, 68, 70–73
Djoser (king), 38–42
Dues, temple, 16
Dynasty 1: *inw* before, 117; *inw* during, 29–35, 41–43, 52, 53, 118
Dynasty 2, *inw* during, 35–38, 41–43, 52, 53, 118
Dynasty 3, 37; *inw* during, 38–43, 52, 53
Dynasty 4, 37; *inw* and, 140n.52
Dynasty 5, 62; *inw* during, 42–51, 53, 72
Dynasty 6: government collapse after, 54; *inw* during, 42–51
Dynasty 9, *inw* during, 54, 55, 143n.13
Dynasty 10, *inw* during, 54, 55
Dynasty 11, *inw* during, 54, 56–60, 62, 63, 65, 66, 80, 87, 88, 118–20
Dynasty 12: *inw* during, 57, 58, 63–76, 80, 83–84, 86–87, 118–20; territorial consolidation during, 64
Dynasty 13, *inw* during, 74–76, 116
Dynasty 18: *inw* during, 107, 115, 120; tomb illustration during, 121–122
Dynasty 19, *inw* during, 120

Ebony, 29
Egypt: economy of, 5, 9, 11–27 (*see also* Merchants, Egyptian); international relations of, 15, 18, 24, 25, 96–99, 101–105, 109–11, 114 (see also *Inw*, from abroad; *Inw*, as war spoils). *See also*

Amarna; Beni Hasan; Bersheh; Illahun; Meir; Memphis; Saqqara; Thebes
Electrum, 102, 104
Eloquent Peasant, The, 87
El-Till hoard. *See* Gold, of Amarna
Embalming, 86
Emendations, misguided text, 140n.56

Famine, 20
Fat, animal, 100
Fellahin, 26
Festivals, 120–22; *inw* and, 68–71, 73, 77–81, 86–88; nature, 87–88. *See also* Heb-Sekhet; New Year Festivals; Sed Festivals; Thoth Festivals
First Intermediate Period: *inw* during, 54–56, 87, 116, 117; tomb desecration during, 49
Firth, Raymond, 9–10
Fisher/Fowler of the Two Ladies, festival of, 120. *See also* King, Egyptian—as Fisher/Fowler of the Two Ladies
Fishing, 71, 73, 122
Food: for deceased, 117–18; royal, 100
Formalism, economic, 9–10; vs. substantivism, 7–8. *See also* Marginal utility theory

Games, memorial, 121
Gift(s), 117; bridal, 99–100; *inw* and royal, 71; *inw* as, 29, 84, 87, 96, 103, 105, 128, 137n.93; *nḏt-ḥr*, 50; social history of, 96–98. See also *Inw*
Gods, Egyptian: kings and, 91–94, 100–103, 114; primacy of, 11
Gold, 14–16, 25, 93, 99, 102, 107, 133n.33, 134n.35; of Amarna, 21–22
Granaries, 12–13, 16–17
Grave goods, 20
Greece, Egypt and, 15

Harkhuf (trader), 24, 44, 136nn.81,84
Hathor Festival, 61
Hatshepsut (queen), 24–25, 91, 93, 101, 108–109, 113
Ḫ̌b (term), 112–13
Ḫ̌b inw, 112–13
Heb-Sekhet, 73
Hekanakht, 12, 13, 80
Helck, W., 16, 18–19
Henou (nobleman), 57
Her-neith (queen), 34
Herskovits, Melville, 9–10
Hetep-Senwosret, Eg., 83, 84
Hides, trade in, 26
Horemheb (as nobleman), 104–105. *See also* Edict of Horemheb *in Index of Egyptian Sources*
Horus (god), 113
Hunting, 70–71, 73, 122

Illahun, Eg., 76, 83, 88, 118. *See also* Illahun papyri *in Index of Egyptian Sources*
Incense, imported, 24–25
Ineni (official), 122
Instructions for Merikare, The, 54, 55

Inw: from abroad, 57, 65, 91–96, 104, 105, 108–11, 114, 119, 121, 142n.5 (see also *Inw*, as war spoils); administration of, 43, 53, 103–14; antiquity of, 3–4; bearers of, 120 (see also *Nḏt*; Women, as offering bearers); defined, 4, 27–28, 42, 45–46, 56, 57, 76, 96 (see also *Inw*, nature of; *Inw*, as term); donors of, 38, 42, 52–53, 111 (see also *Inw*, from abroad); emergence and development of, 29–53; king as central to, 27–29, 31–32, 34, 36, 41–43, 46, 90–103, 117–19, 122 (see also *Inw*, royal uses of; Redistribution, resource—of *inw*); to king's representatives, 94, 95; in literature, 86–88, 115, 116; from nature, 57–58, 61–64, 119–20 (see also Animals, as *inw*; nature of, 11, 82, 95–96, 114, 117; nomarchs and, 54–56, 66–73, 117–20; at royal center, 74–81; as royal privy-purse, 90–94; royal uses of, 84–86; storage of, 111–14, 122; as term, 55, 63, 69, 80, 84, 87–89, 98, 103, 112, 114, 123, 141n.77 (see also *Inw*, defined); translations of, 27, 127–29, 137n.93; uses of, 100–103; as war spoils, 45, 53, 95, 97–98. *See also* Gifts; *Ḫb inw*; *Ms inw*; *M3 inw*; *Šsp inw*
Inw ḥbyt, 77–81
Inw ḥtp-nṯr, 81–82
Inw ḥtp-s-n-wsrt, 82–84
Ivory, 29

Janssen, J. J., 9

Kadish, battle of, 102
Kahun, Eg., 88
Kaplony, Peter, 30–31
Karnak Temple, 92–94, 101
Keftiu, Egypt and, 96, 110
Kemp, Barry, 11–12, 19–23, 136n.75
Khafre, 49
Khakheperre (king), 81, 83
Khnumet-nefer (queen), 78, 80
Khnumhotep II, 21, 67, 68, 70–73, 118
Khnumhotep III, 68, 70
King(s), Egyptian: deference to, 96, 110; as Fisher/Fowler of the Two Ladies, 72, 122; primacy of, 11, 22, 53; Theban, 56. *See also* Coronations; *Inw*, king as central to; Palace; *and individual kings by name*
Kush, Egypt and, 65, 101, 103, 109

Laborers, *inw* for, 100, 103, 114, 118
Land, ownership of Egyptian, 13
Lapis lazuli, 104
Leather, 46, 48
Lebanon, Egypt and, 25
Literature, *inw* in Egyptian, 86–88, 115, 116
Lotus, as symbol, 104, 142n.1

Marginal utility theory, 7, 10, 20, 23

Market(s): Adam Smith on, 9; resource allocation and, 5–6, 8, 9, 11–13
Marxism, 5, 7
Megiddo, Pal., 97
Meir, Eg., 58–61, 68, 70, 88
Memphis, Eg., 57, 71–73, 88, 116
Menkheperre. *See* Thutmose III
Menkheperre–sonb (official), 109
Menkheperrure. *See* Thutmose IV
Mentuhotep III, 57
Mentuhotep IV, 24, 60, 143n.13
Merchants, Egyptian, 13–19, 24, 136n.84. See also *Šwty*
Meret-neith (queen), 34
Merire II, 120–22
Mesekh, 136n.71
Mesopotamia, Polanyi focus on, 132n.17
Middle Kingdom: *inw* during, 56–89, 100, 115–20; royal monuments of, 124; tombs of, 49, 121, 122
Mitr (title), 39, 139n.38
Mittani, Egypt and, 99
Models (historian resource), 123–24
Money: and coinage contrasted, 25; in Egypt, 23, 25–26; Greeks and, 15
Ms inw, 103–106, 111
M3 inw, 106–108
Mummies, 86
Myrrh, 57, 102

Nḏt (*inw*-bearers), 98–99
Nebamun (official), 107–108
Nectanebo I, 15
Neferhotep (scribe), 70
Neferirkare-kakai (funerary complex of), 46, 80
Nefertity (queen), 121
Netjernakht (nomarch), 67, 69
New Kingdom: *inw* during, 42, 45, 49, 90–114, 116–20; royal monuments of, 124
New Year Festival, 61, 70
Niankhkhnum (official), 63, 69
Nobles, *inw* for, 119, 120, 122
Nomarchs: festivals for, 58–61; and *inw*, 54–56, 66–73, 117–20
North, Douglas, 11
Nubia, Egypt and, 24, 95, 101, 105
Nw-jar (symbol), 30, 35, 42

Officials, Egyptian, 50, 65, 120–22. *See also* Nomarchs; Viziers
Oil, vegetable, 20, 100
Old Kingdom: *inw* during, 42–55, 58, 60, 63, 65, 69, 72, 80, 87–89, 115–20; royal monuments of, 124
Oppenheim, A. L., 132n.17

Palace, *inw* for, 74–76, 85, 88, 100, 118, 146n.48
Papyrus (symbol), 31, 36, 142n.1. *See also* Papyri *in Index of Egyptian Sources*
Parades, *inw*-centered, 105–106, 120
Peet, T. E., 23
Peribsen (king), 35, 37
Polanyi, Karl, 5–9, 22, 23, 132n.17; criticisms of, 10–23.

See also Substantivism, economic
Pr (term), 18–19
Ptahhotep II (official), 47–51, 53, 58, 60, 61, 72, 87, 117, 120, 121
Punt, Egypt and, 24, 93, 108, 110, 111
Puyemre (official), 122
Pyramids, 74, 88. *See also* Step Pyramids

Qedes of Gebelein, 12–13, 17
Queens, Egyptian, 34, 85
Quirke, Stephen, 76, 85, 145n.42, 146nn.46,48

Ramesses I, 121
Ramesses II, 16, 102, 111
Ramesses III, 92, 102
Ramesside Period, 105, 120
Reciprocity, goods allocation and, 5, 6, 8–9, 11
Redford, Donald B., 105, 106
Redistribution, resource, 5, 6, 8–9, 11–13, 20, 21; of *inw*, 34–35, 37, 42, 46–55, 58, 61, 66–73, 91, 108, 116, 118, 120–21. *See also* Nobles, *inw* for; Nomarchs, and *inw*; Palace, *inw* for; Temple, *inw* for
Red Land. *See* Punt
Reharakhty (god), 91
Rekhmire (vizier), 110–12, 122
Resources, allocation of, 5–11, 20. *See also* Redistribution, resource
Retenu, Egypt and, 101, 104, 109–10

Salt, 85
Saqqara, Eg., 33–35, 37–41, 48, 60, 72, 87, 118
Scarcity theory, 10
Scharff, A., 146n.46
Seankhkare Mentuhotep, 57
Sed Festivals, 41, 42, 52
Sedge-plant (symbol), 30–31, 36
Sekhemkare (official), 48–51, 53, 58, 62, 63, 117
Sekhem–Senwosret (temple), 84
Sekhet (deified marsh), 122
Senbi (nomarch), 59–61
Senwosret I, 60, 64, 66, 136n.71, 143n.13
Senwosret II, 65, 67, 68, 74, 80, 82, 88
Senwosret III, 13, 65, 67, 70, 74, 76–83, 136n.71
Sethe, K., 140n.56
Sety I, 14–16, 92, 101, 121
Ships. *See* Boats
Silver, 22, 25, 26, 93
Silver, Morris, 11–19, 136n.84
Sirenput II, 65
Slavery, in ancient Egypt, 26
Slaves, *nḏt* as, 98
Smith, Adam, 9
Sobekhotep II, 74–76, 116, 146n.46
Sobekhotep III, 84–85, 146n.46
Soker (festival), 77, 80
Spalinger, Anthony, 85, 146n.48
Šsp inw, 108–11
Step Pyramids, 35, 37, 41, 42
Stone, imported, 24
Stones, precious, 104
Story of Sinuhe, 86, 87

Story of the Shipwrecked Sailor, The, 86, 87
Substantivism, economic, 7–8
Šwty (term), 22
Syria, Egypt and, 18

Taxes, 13–15, 104, 123, 133n.33, 134n.35; on cattle, 67; grain, 21. *See also* Dues, temple
Tefibi of Siut, 54–56
Temple agents, 22
Temples, 82; donors to, 102; *inw* for, 100–103, 118; mortuary, 77–83, 88, 90, 92, 93, 109, 121. *See also* Karnak Temple, *and* Walls, tomb/temple, *in Index of Egyptian Sources*
Theban Tombs, 104, 106
Thebes, Eg., 54, 65, 90, 108, 116, 119
Thoth Festivals, 47, 50, 58, 61, 87, 120–22
Thutmose I, 93, 99, 101
Thutmose II, 93
Thutmose III, 93, 95, 97–99, 101, 104, 106, 107, 109–13, 121, 122. See also *Annals of Thutmose III* in Index of Egyptian Sources
Thutmose IV, 91, 94, 104
Timber, importation of, 25
Tomb of Huy, 106
Tombs, 32–34, 48, 59–60, 63, 65–73, 80, 86–88, 106–108, 112, 113, 117–22, 143n.13; decoration of, 48–49; royal, 32, 33, 35, 53, 58–65, 74, 108–10, 117, 121–22, 142n.1 (*see also* Pyramids); pillaging of, 32. *See also* Theban Tombs, *and* Walls, tomb/temple, *in Index of Egyptian Sources*
Trade: in ancient Egypt, 24–26, 136n.84; and gift-giving contrasted, 96–97; *inw* as, 129. *See also* Barter
Transactions, Egyptian economic, 4–5, 11–28. See also *Inw*; Trade
Transposition, honorific, 30–31, 137–38n.6
Tribute, *inw* as, 45, 129, 137n.93
Turquoise, 104
Tutankhamun (king), 106

Ukhhotep I, 59–61, 70, 73, 121
Ukhhotep II, 68, 70, 72–73

Viziers, 94, 95, 108, 111, 112. *See also* Rekhmire

Wadji (king), 34
Walking legs (symbol), 35
Wenamun (official), 25, 136n.84. See also *Report of Wenamun* in Index of Egyptian Sources
"Window of Appearances," 121
Wine, 100, 108
Women: as offering bearers, 72, 73; as slaves, 26; in tomb decorations, 142n.1
Wrestling, as tomb-art element, 50, 51, 60, 61, 69, 70, 73, 120–21, 143n.15

Yamunedjeh (official), 107–108